# THE LIVING LAMP

# The Living Lamp

Compiled by Pete Pawelek

*Next Generation Disciples* is a two-fold ministry centered first on the development and equipping of the church, directing believers through the three stages of spiritual growth from being a "New Believer" to a "Young Christian" to a "Mature Disciple." The second part of the ministry is worship—and mission-driven, focusing on "Mature Disciples." We aim to work and walk with you through your spiritual growth and to help you achieve what God has planned in your life. Learn more at **www.nextgenerationdisciples.com**.

ISBN-10 0982937237

ISBN-13 9780982937235

*Cover design by* **David Wickersham**.
David may be contacted through the author's website, **www.pastorpete.org**.

*Book design by* **Arc Manor**
Visit their website at **www.arcmanor.com**

℘ ℘

Additional copies of this work and other books by Pete Pawelek may be purchased at
**www.pastorpete.org**

# Contents

# Why The Living Lamp?

The word of God says, "Fix these words of mine in your hearts and minds; tie them as symbols on your hands and bind them on your foreheads. Teach them to your children, talking about them when you sit at home and when you walk along the road, when you lie down and when you get up" (*Deuteronomy 11:18–19*, NIV). Sadly, many parents have come to rely solely on the institution we call church to educate their children about God's word. As a result, there are currently entire generations that know nothing more than surface level Christianity. As a pastor, I have devoted my entire life to serving God's people in His church. Of course, there is nothing wrong with going to church. However, if you think that just by going to church each weekend, you will ever be able to find the full and abundant life that Christ offers, you are wrong. Furthermore, if your desire is that your children or grandchildren might find the richness and extreme pleasure that comes through living a life of obedience to Christ, then we must admit that church is not the answer. God's word alone is what we need; it alone can help individuals of all ages and backgrounds in every circumstance of life. Counting on the church to give your family their entire spiritual diet is both ridiculous and impractical.

Let's deal with the impractical issues first. The average *active* family in our church attends twenty-seven times each year. Of course, some attend more and others less, but on average the active committed families in your church will attend just over half of the Sunday services. This means that all of the work and effort that God's servants put into our children through Sunday school, small groups, youth programs, and other things amounts to about thirty hours of structured time each year. The best-case scenario would only amount to around fifty-two hours a year for a child. A great deal can be accomplished each week during this time at church; however, it is not enough, and it was never God's plan that the church alone would give your children their spiritual education. Now, consider the family. God instituted the family long before the church. Families live, eat, watch TV, play, and work around the house together. While the church only has one hour each week to impact your children, God has given parents 168 hours each week for this purpose.

It is ridiculous to expect that the church alone can educate you or your family. God has graciously given us His Holy Word in written form so that during the week, we might build on what we learn and experience at church. Only when we become actively engaged in worship on a daily basis will we truly grow and mature as disciples. We must return to God's word. We must expose our children to the incredible truths that are contained in its pages as well. The stakes are high and we simply cannot afford to lose another generation to spiritual complacency.

With this in mind, I set out to compile 365 promises, prayers, and challenges directly from God's Holy Word and put them all into *The Living Lamp*. This devotion does not contain a single syllable, much less a sentence, from me or any other human being. From January 1 through December 31, you will find only the word of God on each page. Every day has been designed to encourage dialogue among those in your family. Throughout the year, those who read *The Living Lamp* on a daily basis will be exposed to over two thousand verses from the Bible. Topics about every possible subject and issue will be covered because God's word is alive and it speaks to us as we read it. Each day's passages can be read in a matter of minutes; however, if utilized properly, these precious moments in your day will bring a great reward.

"The word of God is living and active. Sharper than any double-edged sword, it penetrates even to dividing soul and spirit, joints and marrow; it judges the thoughts and attitudes of the heart" (*Hebrews 4:12*, NIV). Second *Timothy 3:16–17* (NIV) proclaims that "All Scripture is God-breathed and is useful for teaching, rebuking, correcting, and training in righteousness, so that the man of God may be thoroughly equipped for every good work." These two verses are only a sample of the many that ultimately prove that God's word is all we need to successfully navigate through the uncharted waters of life. *The Living Lamp* is a tool that any individual, family, or group can use to experience God's word on a daily basis.

Ultimately, this book should be used in conjunction with your regular extended time in God's word. There are many different free Bible reading plans available on the internet. In the Extra Resources section of my personal website, **www.pastorpete.org**, you will find links to many such plans that I would recommend you consider if you do not already have a strategy for reading the Bible on a daily basis.

Many find that starting and ending the day around the table with *The Living Lamp* is the best way to get the most out of this book. Before praying for their meal, families will open *The Living Lamp* and read the promise, prayer, and challenge for the day. Then as they eat and prepare to leave for the day, they simply talk about God's word. Children might ask a question and give parents an opportunity to explain the scripture, teach their children an important lesson, or share a personal testimony. Later that evening, when dinnertime arrives, read the scriptures once again before prayer, then re-cap the day. How did you do with the challenge? Did you see God's promise at work in your life? The discussion will be directed by God's Word and real-life events that are taking place inside the family.

Each day also has a memory verse assignment for the entire family. Every two weeks, a new verse is introduced (see appendix one). Because many are new to scripture memorization, and many children are not developmentally able to memorize long verses, there are three levels to choose from when it comes to your verse for each two-week period. Level one is for the beginner. These verses can be taught to children as young as two years of age. When children are able to speak and actively communicate with others, they should be encouraged to start learning these verses. If you have never memorized scripture, start with level one as well. These short, practical verses will help you learn the discipline of scripture memorization and see the positive effects of it as well. The level-two verses get longer and more complex and are the natural step after you have memorized the verses in level one. Finally, level-three verses consist of longer passages of scripture. While they are more difficult than level two, they are certainly not designed to be impossible to memorize.

Memorize these verses as a family. Hold each other accountable and be consistent. It is best if the entire family actively memorizes scripture on the same level. This allows parents to set the example for their children and to encourage them in this very important discipline. You should practice and apply these verses to your daily lives anytime there is an opportunity. Application is essential. Don't just memorize these passages; look for ways that they apply to your life. Review your verses often. Many families let each member recite one verse from the past before each meal. This keeps older verses fresh in everyone's mind. As you talk about the scriptures for each day, take opportunities to discuss the scriptures you have memorized as well, if it naturally fits into your family conversation.

Parents should set the tone for the family when they open *The Living Lamp* by presenting themselves as learners rather than teachers. Remember, God's word is living and active; it will speak to each family member in a different way. The goal is not to teach, but rather to experience the power of God's word together with others. Everyone should be given an equal opportunity to be involved as well.

Take turns reading, praying, or sharing testimonies. Ask simple and open-ended questions, such as:

1. What did you all think about the promise for today?
2. What will be the most difficult thing about today's challenge?
3. What part of the prayer scripture did you enjoy most?
4. What did our readings today teach us about God?
5. What did our passages teach us about ourselves?
6. Was there anything in today's reading that made you think twice?
7. How do these verses apply to our lives?
8. What do you think this means?
9. Why do you think God wanted us to know that?
10. Which of our past memory verses did that passage remind you of?

When we take the time to read God's word together as a family, the results are amazing. However, they will not be instant. If you and your family have not been actively involved in reading and experiencing God's word together, be patient. Don't be surprised if the devil mounts many attacks to frustrate your time together in God's word. Children might embrace the experience at first and then go through phases of rejecting God's word. My two-year-old son, for example, will soak up any memory verse he is challenged with for months. Then, with no explanation, he will just refuse to learn any more or practice his older verses. We do not make him, bribe him, or pressure him in any way. Instead, my wife and I remain faithful in our own efforts to memorize God's word. In a short amount of time, he generally once again becomes willing to take part in scripture memorization. Be patient, and set the example for your children. They will learn more by watching you than you think. May God light your path and bless your life through *The Living Lamp*.

> *How sweet are your words to my taste, sweeter than honey to my mouth! I gain understanding from your precepts; therefore I hate every wrong path.* **Your word is a lamp to my feet and a light for my path.** *I have taken an oath and confirmed it, that I will follow your righteous laws. I have suffered much; preserve my life, O LORD, according to your word.* **Psalms 119:103–107** NIV

# January

## ᏏᎤ JANUARY 1 ᏟᏪ

*Memory Verse 1*

**PROMISE:** So then, don't worry saying, 'What will we eat?' or 'What will we drink?' or 'What will we wear?' ³²For the unconverted pursue these things, and your heavenly Father knows that you need them. *Matthew 6:31–32* NET

**PRAYER:** The Lamb who was slaughtered is worthy to receive power and riches and wisdom and strength and honor and glory and blessing! *Revelation 5:12* HCSB

**CHALLENGE:** And this is his command: to believe in the name of his Son, Jesus Christ, and to love one another as he commanded us. *1 John 3:23* NIV

## ᏏᎤ JANUARY 2 ᏟᏪ

*Memory Verse 1*

**PROMISE:** God is not a man, so he does not lie. He is not human, so he does not change his mind. Has he ever spoken and failed to act? Has he ever promised and not carried it through? *Numbers 23:19* NLT

**PRAYER:** Certainly my tongue does not frame a word without you, O LORD, being thoroughly aware of it. ⁵You squeeze me in from behind and in front; you place your hand on me. ⁶Your knowledge is beyond my comprehension; it is so far beyond me, I am unable to fathom it. *Psalms 139:4–6* NET

**CHALLENGE:** I appeal to you therefore, brothers, by the mercies of God, to present your bodies as a living sacrifice, holy and acceptable to God, which is your spiritual worship. *Romans 12:1* ESV

## ℰᴏ JANUARY 3 ℭᴚ

### *Memory Verse 1*

**PROMISE:** He is the image of the invisible God, the firstborn over all creation. ¹⁶For by Him all things were created that are in heaven and that are on earth, visible and invisible, whether thrones or dominions or principalities or powers. All things were created through Him and for Him. ¹⁷And He is before all things, and in Him all things consist. *Colossians 1:15–17* NKJV

**PRAYER:** Finally, brothers and sisters, whatever is true, whatever is worthy of respect, whatever is just, whatever is pure, whatever is lovely, whatever is commendable, if something is excellent or praiseworthy, think about these things. *Philippians 4:8* NET

**CHALLENGE:** Brothers and sisters, stop slandering each other. Those who slander and judge other believers slander and judge God's teachings. If you judge God's teachings, you are no longer following them. Instead, you are judging them. ¹²There is only one teacher and judge. He is able to save or destroy you. So who are you to judge your neighbor? *James 4:11–12* GWORD

## ℰᴏ JANUARY 4 ℭᴚ

### *Memory Verse 1*

**PROMISE:** For I am sure of this very thing, that the one who began a good work in you will perfect it until the day of Christ Jesus. *Philippians 1:6* NET

**PRAYER:** "Let all their wickedness come before You, And do to them as You have done to me For all my transgressions; For my sighs are many, And my heart is faint." *Lamentations 1:22* NKJV

**CHALLENGE:** Don't let sexual sin, perversion of any kind, or greed even be mentioned among you. This is not appropriate behavior for God's holy people. ⁴It's not right that dirty stories, foolish talk, or obscene jokes should be mentioned among you either. *Ephesians 5:3–4* GWORD

# ෨ JANUARY 5 ෬

*Memory Verse 1*

**PROMISE:** "So I tell you: Ask, and it will be given to you; seek, and you will find; knock, and the door will be opened for you. ¹⁰For everyone who asks receives, and the one who seeks finds, and to the one who knocks, the door will be opened. ¹¹What father among you, if your son asks for a fish, will give him a snake instead of a fish? *Luke 11:9–11* NET

**PRAYER:** "I love You, O LORD, my strength." ²The LORD is my rock and my fortress and my deliverer, My God, my rock, in whom I take refuge; My shield and the horn of my salvation, my stronghold. *Psalms 18:1–2* NAS95

**CHALLENGE:** Immediately Jesus spoke to them. "Have courage! It is I. Don't be afraid." ²⁸"Lord, if it's You," Peter answered Him, "command me to come to You on the water." ²⁹"Come!" He said. And climbing out of the boat, Peter started walking on the water and came toward Jesus. ³⁰But when he saw the strength of the wind, he was afraid. And beginning to sink he cried out, "Lord, save me!" ³¹Immediately Jesus reached out His hand, caught hold of him, and said to him, "You of little faith, why did you doubt?" *Matthew 14:27–31* HCSB

# ෨ JANUARY 6 ෬

*Memory Verse 1*

**PROMISE:** There are many dwelling places in my Father's house. Otherwise, I would have told you, because I am going away to make ready a place for you. ³And if I go and make ready a place for you, I will come again and take you to be with me, so that where I am you may be too. *John 14:2–3* NET

**PRAYER:** The sacrifice of the wicked is an abomination to the LORD, but the prayer of the upright is acceptable to him. *Proverbs 15:8* ESV

**CHALLENGE:** As you therefore have received Christ Jesus the Lord, so walk in Him, ⁷rooted and built up in Him and established in the faith, as you have been taught, abounding in it with thanksgiving. *Colossians 2:6–7* NKJV

## ஐ JANUARY 7 ‖

*Memory Verse 1*

**PROMISE:** But the LORD said to Samuel, "Do not look on his appearance or on the height of his stature, because I have rejected him. For the LORD sees not as man sees: man looks on the outward appearance, but the LORD looks on the heart." *1 Samuel 16:7* ESV

**PRAYER:** I pray that according to the wealth of his glory he may grant you to be strengthened with power through his Spirit in the inner person, ¹⁷that Christ may dwell in your hearts through faith, so that, because you have been rooted and grounded in love, ¹⁸you may be able to comprehend with all the saints what is the breadth and length and height and depth, ¹⁹and thus to know the love of Christ that surpasses knowledge, so that you may be filled up to all the fullness of God. *Ephesians 3:16–19* NET

**CHALLENGE:** David also told his son Solomon, "Be strong and courageous, and do the work. Don't be afraid or terrified. The Lord God, my God, will be with you. He will not abandon you before all the work on the Lord's temple is finished. *1 Chronicles 28:20* GWORD

## ❧ JANUARY 8 ❧

*Memory Verse 1*

**PROMISE:** For behold, the LORD is coming out of His place; He will come down And tread on the high places of the earth. ⁴The mountains will melt under Him, And the valleys will split Like wax before the fire, Like waters poured down a steep place. *Micah 1:3–4* NKJV

**PRAYER:** Answer me quickly, LORD! My strength is fading. Do not reject me, or I will join those descending into the grave. ⁸May I hear about your loyal love in the morning, for I trust in you. Show me the way I should go, because I long for you. ⁹Rescue me from my enemies, O LORD! I run to you for protection. ¹⁰Teach me to do what pleases you, for you are my God. May your kind presence lead me into a level land. ¹¹O LORD, for the sake of your reputation, revive me! Because of your justice, rescue me from trouble! *Psalms 143:7–11* NET

**CHALLENGE:** Whoever forgives an offense seeks love, but whoever keeps bringing up the issue separates the closest of friends. *Proverbs 17:9* GWORD

## ❧ JANUARY 9 ❧

*Memory Verse 1*

**PROMISE:** But above all pursue his kingdom and righteousness, and all these things will be given to you as well. *Matthew 6:33* NET

**PRAYER:** Worship the LORD in the splendor of holiness; ³⁰tremble before him, all the earth; yes, the world is established; it shall never be moved. *1 Chronicles 16:29–30* ESV

**CHALLENGE:** Shout triumphantly to the LORD, all the earth. ²Serve the LORD with gladness; come before Him with joyful songs. ³Acknowledge that Yahweh is God. He made us, and we are His—His people, the sheep of His pasture. ⁴Enter His gates with thanksgiving and His courts with praise. Give thanks to Him and praise His name. *Psalms 100:1–4* HCSB

# ❧ JANUARY 10 ❧

*Memory Verse 1*

**PROMISE:** Pay attention to this! You're saying, "Today or tomorrow we will go into some city, stay there a year, conduct business, and make money." ¹⁴You don't know what will happen tomorrow. What is life? You are a mist that is seen for a moment and then disappears. ¹⁵Instead, you should say, "If the Lord wants us to, we will live and carry out our plans." *James 4:13–15* GWORD

**PRAYER:** Not to us, O LORD, not to us but to your name be the glory, because of your love and faithfulness. *Psalms 115:1* NIV

**CHALLENGE:** For you know what commands we gave you through the Lord Jesus. ³For this is God's will: that you become holy, that you keep away from sexual immorality, ⁴that each of you know how to possess his own body in holiness and honor, ⁵not in lustful passion like the Gentiles who do not know God. *1 Thessalonians 4:2–5* NET

# ❧ JANUARY 11 ❧

*Memory Verse 1*

**PROMISE:** For the Lord himself will come down from heaven with a shout of command, with the voice of the archangel, and with the trumpet of God, and the dead in Christ will rise first. ¹⁷Then we who are alive, who are left, will be suddenly caught up together with them in the clouds to meet the Lord in the air. And so we will always be with the Lord. *1 Thessalonians 4:16–17* NET

**PRAYER:** Bless the LORD, O my soul; And all that is within me, bless His holy name! *Psalms 103:1* NKJV

**CHALLENGE:** "Be careful not to do your 'acts of righteousness' before men, to be seen by them. If you do, you will have no reward from your Father in heaven. *Matthew 6:1* NIV

## ℘ JANUARY 12 ℃

*Memory Verse 1*

**PROMISE:** You can be sure that using people or religion or things just for what you can get out of them—the usual variations on idolatry—will get you nowhere, and certainly nowhere near the kingdom of Christ, the kingdom of God. *Ephesians 5:5* MESSAGE

**PRAYER:** Call on Me in a day of trouble; I will rescue you, and you will honor Me." *Psalms 50:15* HCSB

**CHALLENGE:** Now we ask you, brothers and sisters, to acknowledge those who labor among you and preside over you in the Lord and admonish you, ¹³and to esteem them most highly in love because of their work. Be at peace among yourselves. *1 Thessalonians 5:12–13* NET

## ℘ JANUARY 13 ℃

*Memory Verse 1*

**PROMISE:** With the faithful You prove Yourself faithful; with the blameless man You prove Yourself blameless; ²⁶with the pure You prove Yourself pure, but with the crooked You prove Yourself shrewd. *Psalms 18:25–26* HCSB

**PRAYER:** Now to him who by the power that is working within us is able to do far beyond all that we ask or think, ²¹to him be the glory in the church and in Christ Jesus to all generations, forever and ever. Amen. *Ephesians 3:20–21* NET

**CHALLENGE:** And Peter said to them, "Repent and be baptized every one of you in the name of Jesus Christ for the forgiveness of your sins, and you will receive the gift of the Holy Spirit. *Acts 2:38* ESV

## ℘ JANUARY 14 ℂ

*Memory Verse 1*

**PROMISE:** There is therefore now no condemnation to those who are in Christ Jesus, who do not walk according to the flesh, but according to the Spirit. *Romans 8:1* NKJV

**PRAYER:** How great is your goodness, which you have stored up for those who fear you, which you bestow in the sight of men on those who take refuge in you. *Psalms 31:19* NIV

**CHALLENGE:** "Bring the entire tithe into the storehouse so that there may be food in my temple. Test me in this matter," says the LORD who rules over all, "to see if I will not open for you the windows of heaven and pour out for you a blessing until there is no room for it all. *Malachi 3:10* NET

## ℘ JANUARY 15 ℂ

*Memory Verse 1*

**PROMISE:** There shall be no night there: They need no lamp nor light of the sun, for the Lord God gives them light. And they shall reign forever and ever. *Revelation 22:5* NKJV

**PRAYER:** He is the payment for our sins, and not only for our sins, but also for the sins of the whole world. *1 John 2:2* GWORD

**CHALLENGE:** Always rejoice, [17]constantly pray, [18]in everything give thanks. For this is God's will for you in Christ Jesus. *1 Thessalonians 5:16–18* NET

## ℘ JANUARY 16 ℂ

*Memory Verse 1*

**PROMISE:** And while they looked steadfastly toward heaven as He went up, behold, two men stood by them in white apparel,

¹¹who also said, "Men of Galilee, why do you stand gazing up into heaven? This same Jesus, who was taken up from you into heaven, will so come in like manner as you saw Him go into heaven." *Acts 1:10–11* NKJV

**PRAYER:** And in this regard we pray for you always, that our God will make you worthy of his calling and fulfill by his power your every desire for goodness and every work of faith, ¹²that the name of our Lord Jesus may be glorified in you, and you in him, according to the grace of our God and the Lord Jesus Christ. *2 Thessalonians 1:11–12* NET

**CHALLENGE:** Do not withhold good from those who deserve it, when it is in your power to act. ²⁸Do not say to your neighbor, "Come back later; I'll give it tomorrow"—when you now have it with you. *Proverbs 3:27–28* NIV

## ஐ JANUARY **17** ൏

*Memory Verse 2*

**PROMISE:** Finally, brothers and sisters, rejoice, set things right, be encouraged, agree with one another, live in peace, and the God of love and peace will be with you. *2 Corinthians 13:11* NET

**PRAYER:** Grace, mercy and peace from God the Father and from Jesus Christ, the Father's Son, will be with us in truth and love. *2 John 1:3* NIV

**CHALLENGE:** Follow my rules, and live by my standards. I am the Lord your God. ⁵Live by my standards, and obey my rules. You will have life through them. I am the Lord. *Leviticus 18:4–5* GWORD

## ஐ JANUARY **18** ൏

*Memory Verse 2*

**PROMISE:** Enoch, who lived in the seventh generation after Adam, prophesied about these people. He said, "Listen! The Lord is coming with countless thousands of his holy ones ¹⁵to execute judgment on the people of the world. He will convict every person of all the ungodly things they have done and for all the insults that ungodly sinners have spoken against him." *Jude 1:14–15* NLT

**PRAYER:** Now may the Lord of peace himself give you peace at all times and in every way. The Lord be with you all. ¹⁷I, Paul, write this greeting with my own hand, which is how I write in every letter. ¹⁸The grace of our Lord Jesus Christ be with you all. *2 Thessalonians 3:16–18* NET

**CHALLENGE:** Do not gloat over your brother in the day of his calamity; do not rejoice over the people of Judah in the day of their destruction; do not boastfully mock in the day of distress. *Obadiah 1:12* HCSB

# ℰ JANUARY 19 ℛ

*Memory Verse 2*

**PROMISE:** Therefore do not worry about tomorrow, for tomorrow will worry about itself. Each day has enough trouble of its own. *Matthew 6:34* NIV

**PRAYER:** But you, brothers and sisters, do not grow weary in doing what is right. *2 Thessalonians 3:13* NET

**CHALLENGE:** But be doers of the word, and not hearers only, deceiving yourselves. ²³For if anyone is a hearer of the word and not a doer, he is like a man observing his natural face in a mirror; ²⁴for he observes himself, goes away, and immediately forgets what kind of man he was. ²⁵But he who looks into the perfect law of liberty and continues in it, and is not a forgetful hearer but a doer of the work, this one will be blessed in what he does. *James 1:22–25* NKJV

## ෨ JANUARY 20 ෬

*Memory Verse 2*

**PROMISE:** Go and gather the elders of Israel together and say to them, 'The LORD, the God of your fathers, the God of Abraham, of Isaac, and of Jacob, has appeared to me, saying, "I have observed you and what has been done to you in Egypt, ¹⁷and I promise that I will bring you up out of the affliction of Egypt to the land of the Canaanites, the Hittites, the Amorites, the Perizzites, the Hivites, and the Jebusites, a land flowing with milk and honey."' *Exodus 3:16–17* ESV

**PRAYER:** Finally, pray for us, brothers and sisters, that the Lord's message may spread quickly and be honored as in fact it was among you, ²and that we may be delivered from perverse and evil people. For not all have faith. ³But the Lord is faithful, and he will strengthen you and protect you from the evil one. *2 Thessalonians 3:1–3* NET

**CHALLENGE:** I made your rebellious acts disappear like a thick cloud and your sins like the morning mist. Come back to me, because I have reclaimed you. *Isaiah 44:22* GWORD

## ෨ JANUARY 21 ෬

*Memory Verse 2*

**PROMISE:** Your sun will no longer go down, nor will your moon disappear. The Lord will be your everlasting light, and your days of sadness will be over. *Isaiah 60:20* GWORD

**PRAYER:** O LORD, you examine me and know. ²You know when I sit down and when I get up; even from far away you understand my motives. ³You carefully observe me when I travel or when I lie down to rest; you are aware of everything I do. *Psalms 139:1–3* NET

**CHALLENGE:** Then Jesus said to them, "Follow Me, and I will make you become fishers of men." ¹⁸They immediately left their nets and followed Him. *Mark 1:17–18* NKJV

## ℬ JANUARY 22 ℭ

*Memory Verse 2*

**PROMISE:** Come to me, all you who are weary and burdened, and I will give you rest. <sup>29</sup>Take my yoke on you and learn from me, because I am gentle and humble in heart, and you will find rest for your souls. *Matthew 11:28–29* NET

**PRAYER:** I call upon the LORD, who is worthy to be praised, and I am saved from my enemies. *Psalms 18:3* ESV

**CHALLENGE:** We must not become conceited, provoking one another, envying one another. *Galatians 5:26* HCSB

## ℬ JANUARY 23 ℭ

*Memory Verse 2*

**PROMISE:** The eyes of the LORD are in every place, keeping watch on the evil and the good. *Proverbs 15:3* ESV

**PRAYER:** I constantly remember you in my prayers night and day when I thank God, whom I serve with a clear conscience as my ancestors did. <sup>4</sup>I remember your tears and want to see you so that I can be filled with happiness. <sup>5</sup>I'm reminded of how sincere your faith is. That faith first lived in your grandmother Lois and your mother Eunice. I'm convinced that it also lives in you. *2 Timothy 1:3–5* GWORD

**CHALLENGE:** I, therefore, the prisoner for the Lord, urge you to live worthily of the calling with which you have been called, <sup>2</sup>with all humility and gentleness, with patience, bearing with one another in love, <sup>3</sup>making every effort to keep the unity of the Spirit in the bond of peace. *Ephesians 4:1–3* NET

## ᔥ JANUARY 24 ᘛ

*Memory Verse 2*

**PROMISE:** You will be confident, because there is hope. You will look carefully about and lie down in safety. ¹⁹You will lie down without fear, and many will seek your favor. ²⁰But the sight of the wicked will fail. Their way of escape will be cut off, and their only hope is their last breath. *Job 11:18–20* HCSB

**PRAYER:** "Thus let all Your enemies perish, O LORD! But let those who love Him be like the sun When it comes out in full strength." So the land had rest for forty years. *Judges 5:31* NKJV

**CHALLENGE:** Trust in the LORD and do what is right! Settle in the land and maintain your integrity! *Psalms 37:3* NET

## ᔥ JANUARY 25 ᘛ

*Memory Verse 2*

**PROMISE:** The Devil who deceived them was thrown into the lake of fire and sulfur where the beast and the false prophet are, and they will be tormented day and night forever and ever. *Revelation 20:10* HCSB

**PRAYER:** If I were to say, "Certainly the darkness will cover me, and the light will turn to night all around me," ¹²even the darkness is not too dark for you to see, and the night is as bright as day; darkness and light are the same to you. ¹³Certainly you made my mind and heart; you wove me together in my mother's womb. *Psalms 139:11–13* NET

**CHALLENGE:** But the angel of the Lord by night opened the prison doors, and brought them forth, and said, ²⁰Go, stand and speak in the temple to the people all the words of this life. *Acts 5:19–20* KJV

## ℘ JANUARY 26 ☙

*Memory Verse 2*

**PROMISE:** Jesus began by telling them: "Watch out that no one deceives you. ⁶Many will come in My name, saying, 'I am He,' and they will deceive many. ⁷When you hear of wars and rumors of wars, don't be alarmed; these things must take place, but the end is not yet. ⁸For nation will rise up against nation, and kingdom against kingdom. There will be earthquakes in various places, and famines. These are the beginning of birth pains. *Mark 13:5–8* HCSB

**PRAYER:** For the LORD is a great God, and a great King above all gods. ⁴In his hand are the depths of the earth; the heights of the mountains are his also. ⁵The sea is his, for he made it, and his hands formed the dry land. *Psalms 95:3–5* ESV

**CHALLENGE:** A friend always loves, and a brother is born to share trouble. *Proverbs 17:17* GWORD

## ℘ JANUARY 27 ☙

*Memory Verse 2*

**PROMISE:** This is what the Lord says: Cursed is the person who trusts humans, who makes flesh and blood his strength and whose heart turns away from the Lord. *Jeremiah 17:5* GWORD

**PRAYER:** "I cried out to the LORD in my great trouble, and he answered me. I called to you from the land of the dead, and LORD, you heard me! ³You threw me into the ocean depths, and I sank down to the heart of the sea. The mighty waters engulfed me; I was buried beneath your wild and stormy waves. ⁴Then I said, 'O LORD, you have driven me from your presence. Yet I will look once more toward your holy Temple.' ⁵"I sank beneath the waves, and the waters closed over me. Seaweed wrapped itself around my head. ⁶I sank down to the very roots of the mountains. I was imprisoned in the earth, whose gates lock shut forever. But you, O LORD my God, snatched me from the jaws of death! ⁷As my life was slipping away,

I remembered the LORD. And my earnest prayer went out to you in your holy Temple. ⁸Those who worship false gods turn their backs on all God's mercies. ⁹But I will offer sacrifices to you with songs of praise, and I will fulfill all my vows. For my salvation comes from the LORD alone." ¹⁰Then the LORD ordered the fish to spit Jonah out onto the beach. *Jonah 2:2–10* NLT

**CHALLENGE:** Dear children, keep yourselves from idols. *1 John 5:21* NIV

## ඏ JANUARY 28 ભ

*Memory Verse 2*

**PROMISE:** Each person's ways are clearly seen by the Lord, and he surveys all his actions. *Proverbs 5:21* GWORD

**PRAYER:** For God did not send his Son into the world to condemn the world, but in order that the world might be saved through him. *John 3:17–18* ESV

**CHALLENGE:** When I am afraid, I trust in you. ⁴In God—I boast in his promise—in God I trust, I am not afraid. What can mere men do to me? *Psalms 56:3–4* NET

## ඏ JANUARY 29 ભ

*Memory Verse 2*

**PROMISE:** I will certainly save you. You will not fall victim to violence. You will escape with your life because you trust in me. I, the LORD, affirm it!" *Jeremiah 39:18* NET

**PRAYER:** Be exalted, O God, above the heavens; let your glory be over all the earth. *Psalms 57:11* NIV

**CHALLENGE:** Seek good and not evil, That you may live; So the LORD God of hosts will be with you, As you have spoken. ¹⁵Hate evil, love good; Establish justice in the gate. It may be that the

LORD God of hosts Will be gracious to the remnant of Joseph. *Amos 5:14–15* NKJV

## ೕ JANUARY 30 ಝ

*Memory Verse 2*

**PROMISE:** Remember these things, Jacob: You are my servant, Israel. I formed you; you are my servant. Israel, I will not forget you. *Isaiah 44:21* GWORD

**PRAYER:** How difficult it is for me to fathom your thoughts about me, O God! How vast is their sum total! [18]If I tried to count them, they would outnumber the grains of sand. Even if I finished counting them, I would still have to contend with you. *Psalms 139:17–18* NET

**CHALLENGE:** that if you confess with your mouth Jesus as Lord, and believe in your heart that God raised Him from the dead, you will be saved; [10]for with the heart a person believes, resulting in righteousness, and with the mouth he confesses, resulting in salvation. *Romans 10:9–10* NAS95

## ೕ JANUARY 31 ಝ

*Memory Verse 3*

**PROMISE:** The LORD is good—indeed, he is a fortress in time of distress, and he protects those who seek refuge in him. *Nahum 1:7* NET

**PRAYER:** I will give you sincere thanks, when I learn your just regulations. [8]I will keep your statutes. Do not completely abandon me! *Psalms 119:7–8* NET

**CHALLENGE:** To the weak I became weak, in order to win the weak. I have become all things to all people, so that I may by every possible means save some. *1 Corinthians 9:22* HCSB

# February

## ဩ FEBRUARY 1 ભ

*Memory Verse 3*

**PROMISE:** How blessed are those whose actions are blameless, who obey the law of the LORD. *Psalms 119:1* NET

**PRAYER:** Then in a night vision the mystery was revealed to Daniel. So Daniel praised the God of heaven, ²⁰saying, "Let the name of God be praised forever and ever, for wisdom and power belong to him. ²¹He changes times and seasons, deposing some kings and establishing others. He gives wisdom to the wise; he imparts knowledge to those with understanding; ²²he reveals deep and hidden things. He knows what is in the darkness, and light resides with him. *Daniel 2:19–22* NET

**CHALLENGE:** And this is love: that we walk in obedience to his commands. As you have heard from the beginning, his command is that you walk in love. *2 John 1:6* NIV

## ဩ FEBRUARY 2 ભ

*Memory Verse 3*

**PROMISE:** Whoever believes in the Son has eternal life; whoever does not obey the Son shall not see life, but the wrath of God remains on him. *John 3:36* ESV

**PRAYER:** Keep watching and praying that you may not come into temptation; the spirit is willing, but the flesh is weak." ³⁹Again He went away and prayed, saying the same words. ⁴⁰And again He came and found them sleeping, for their eyes were very heavy; and they did not know what to answer Him. *Mark 14:38–40* NAS95

**CHALLENGE:** Starting a quarrel is ‹like› opening a floodgate, so stop before the argument gets out of control. *Proverbs 17:14* GWORD

## ℰ❧ FEBRUARY 3 ☜❧

*Memory Verse 3*

**PROMISE:** Anxiety in a man's heart weighs it down, But a good word makes it glad. *Proverbs 12:25* NAS95

**PRAYER:** And they sang a new song: You are worthy to take the scroll and to open its seals, because You were slaughtered, and You redeemed people for God by Your blood from every tribe and language and people and nation. ¹⁰You made them a kingdom and priests to our God, and they will reign on the earth. *Revelation 5:9–10* HCSB

**CHALLENGE:** Therefore lay aside all filthiness and overflow of wickedness, and receive with meekness the implanted word, which is able to save your souls. *James 1:21* NKJV

## ℰ❧ FEBRUARY 4 ☜❧

*Memory Verse 3*

**PROMISE:** "Behold, I am coming quickly! Blessed is he who keeps the words of the prophecy of this book." *Revelation 22:7* NKJV

**PRAYER:** Turn toward me and extend mercy to me, as you typically do to your loyal followers. ¹³³Direct my steps by your word! Do not let any sin dominate me! *Psalms 119:132–133* NET

**CHALLENGE:** Now those who belong to Christ Jesus have crucified the flesh with its passions and desires. ²⁵Since we live by the Spirit, we must also follow the Spirit. *Galatians 5:24–26* HCSB

## ℘ FEBRUARY 5 ℘

*Memory Verse 3*

**PROMISE:** So do not worry, saying, 'What shall we eat?' or 'What shall we drink?' or 'What shall we wear?' ³²For the pagans run after all these things, and your heavenly Father knows that you need them. *Matthew 6:31–32* NIV

**PRAYER:** Then we will not turn back from You; Revive us, and we will call upon Your name. ¹⁹Restore us, O LORD God of hosts; Cause Your face to shine, And we shall be saved! *Psalms 80:18–19* NKJV

**CHALLENGE:** ²Don't become like the people of this world. Instead, change the way you think. Then you will always be able to determine what God really wants—what is good, pleasing, and perfect. *Romans 12:1–2* GWORD

## ℘ FEBRUARY 6 ℘

*Memory Verse 3*

**PROMISE:** An undisciplined, self-willed life is puny; an obedient, God-willed life is spacious. *Proverbs 15:32* MESSAGE

**PRAYER:** Let me not be put to shame, O LORD, for I have cried out to you; but let the wicked be put to shame and lie silent in the grave. *Psalms 31:17* NIV

**CHALLENGE:** "Arise! For this matter is your responsibility, but we will be with you; be courageous and act." *Ezra 10:4* NAS95

## ℘ FEBRUARY 7 ℘

*Memory Verse 3*

**PROMISE:** The way of the godly leads to life; that path does not lead to death. *Proverbs 12:28* NLT

**PRAYER:** Now in the morning, having risen a long while before daylight, He went out and departed to a solitary place; and there He prayed. *Mark 1:35* NKJV

**CHALLENGE:** Therefore, my dear brothers, stand firm. Let nothing move you. Always give yourselves fully to the work of the Lord, because you know that your labor in the Lord is not in vain. *1 Corinthians 15:58* NIV

## ℰ℧ FEBRUARY 8 ℭℛ

### *Memory Verse 3*

**PROMISE:** Blessed is the person who trusts the Lord. The Lord will be his confidence. ⁸He will be like a tree that is planted by water. It will send its roots down to a stream. It will not be afraid in the heat of summer. Its leaves will turn green. It will not be anxious during droughts. It will not stop producing fruit. *Jeremiah 17:7–8* GWORD

**PRAYER:** In my distress I called upon the LORD, And cried out to my God; He heard my voice from His temple, And my cry came before Him, even to His ears. *Psalms 18:6* NKJV

**CHALLENGE:** So Jesus said to the Jews who had believed Him, "If you continue in My word, you really are My disciples. ³²You will know the truth, and the truth will set you free." *John 8:31–32* HCSB

## ℰ℧ FEBRUARY 9 ℭℛ

### *Memory Verse 3*

**PROMISE:** A wise child accepts a parent's discipline; a mocker refuses to listen to correction. *Proverbs 13:1* NLT

**PRAYER:** Greet one another with a holy kiss. All of God's holy people greet you. ¹³May the Lord Jesus Christ's good will, God's love, and the Holy Spirit's presence be with all of you! *2 Corinthians 13:12–13* GWORD

**CHALLENGE:** And the LORD spoke to Moses, saying, ²"Speak to all the congregation of the children of Israel, and say to them: 'You shall be holy, for I the LORD your God am holy. *Leviticus 19:1–2* NKJV

## ෨ FEBRUARY 10 ൙

*Memory Verse 3*

**PROMISE:** "Now My soul is troubled, and what shall I say? 'Father, save Me from this hour'? But for this purpose I came to this hour. ²⁸Father, glorify Your name." Then a voice came from heaven, saying, "I have both glorified it and will glorify it again." *John 12:27–28* NKJV

**PRAYER:** First, I thank my God through Jesus Christ for all of you because the news of your faith is being reported in all the world. ⁹For God, whom I serve with my spirit in telling the good news about His Son, is my witness that I constantly mention you, ¹⁰always asking in my prayers that if it is somehow in God's will, I may now at last succeed in coming to you. *Romans 1:8–10* HCSB

**CHALLENGE:** Trust in the LORD with all your heart, and do not rely on your own understanding. *Proverbs 3:5* NET

## ෨ FEBRUARY 11 ൙

*Memory Verse 3*

**PROMISE:** Then they will be My people, and I will be their God. ²¹But as for those whose hearts pursue their desire for detestable things and practices, I will bring their actions down on their own heads." This is the declaration of the Lord GOD. *Ezekiel 11:20–21* HCSB

**PRAYER:** O LORD, our Lord, how majestic is your name in all the earth! *Psalms 8:9* NIV

**CHALLENGE:** I want women to show their beauty by dressing in appropriate clothes that are modest and respectable. Their beauty will be shown by what they do, not by their hair styles or the gold jewelry, pearls, or expensive clothes they wear. ¹⁰This is what is proper for women who claim to have reverence for God. *1 Timothy 2:9–10* GWORD

## ℘ FEBRUARY 12 ℘

### *Memory Verse 3*

**PROMISE:** Therefore, if the Son sets you free, you really will be free. John 8:36 HCSB

**PRAYER:** I urge, then, first of all, that requests, prayers, intercession and thanksgiving be made for everyone—²for kings and all those in authority, that we may live peaceful and quiet lives in all godliness and holiness. ³This is good, and pleases God our Savior, ⁴who wants all men to be saved and to come to a knowledge of the truth. *1 Timothy 2:1–4* NIV

**CHALLENGE:** I want you to show love, not offer sacrifices. I want you to know me more than I want burnt offerings. *Hosea 6:6* NLT

## ℘ FEBRUARY 13 ℘

### *Memory Verse 3*

**PROMISE:** Better to be criticized by a wise person than to be praised by a fool. *Ecclesiastes 7:5* NLT

**PRAYER:** Your rules are marvelous. Therefore I observe them. ¹³⁰Your instructions are a doorway through which light shines. They give insight to the untrained. ¹³¹I open my mouth and pant, because I long for your commands. *Psalms 119:129–131* NET

**CHALLENGE:** "But you, be on your guard! They will hand you over to sanhedrins, and you will be flogged in the synagogues. You will stand before governors and kings because of Me, as a witness to them. ¹⁰And the good news must first be proclaimed to all nations. ¹¹So when they arrest you and hand you over, don't worry beforehand what you will say. On the contrary, whatever is given to you in that hour—say it. For it isn't you speaking, but the Holy Spirit. *Mark 13:9–11* HCSB

## ℬ FEBRUARY **14** ℛ

*Memory Verse 4*

**PROMISE:** And Jesus cried out with a loud voice, and breathed His last. ³⁸Then the veil of the temple was torn in two from top to bottom. ³⁹So when the centurion, who stood opposite Him, saw that He cried out like this and breathed His last, he said, "Truly this Man was the Son of God!" *Mark 15:37–39* NKJV

**PRAYER:** You have filled my heart with greater joy than when their grain and new wine abound. ⁸I will lie down and sleep in peace, for you alone, O LORD, make me dwell in safety. *Psalms 4:7–8* NIV

**CHALLENGE:** Brothers, if someone is caught in any wrongdoing, you who are spiritual should restore such a person with a gentle spirit, watching out for yourselves so you also won't be tempted. *Galatians 6:1* HCSB

## ℬ FEBRUARY **15** ℛ

*Memory Verse 4*

**PROMISE:** There are six things which the LORD hates, Yes, seven which are an abomination to Him: ¹⁷Haughty eyes, a lying tongue, And hands that shed innocent blood, ¹⁸A heart that devises wicked plans, Feet that run rapidly to evil, ¹⁹A false witness who utters lies, And one who spreads strife among brothers. *Proverbs 6:16–19* NAS95

**PRAYER:** God showed how much he loved us by sending his one and only Son into the world so that we might have eternal life through him. ¹⁰This is real love—not that we loved God, but that he loved us and sent his Son as a sacrifice to take away our sins. *1 John 4:9–10* NLT

**CHALLENGE:** Therefore, rid yourselves of all malice and all deceit, hypocrisy, envy, and slander of every kind. *1 Peter 2:1* NIV

## ℰ❧ FEBRUARY 16 ❦

*Memory Verse 4*

**PROMISE:** How can a young person maintain a pure life? By guarding it according to your instructions! *Psalms 119:9* NET

**PRAYER:** You want what you don't have, so you commit murder. You're determined to have things, but you can't get what you want. You quarrel and fight. You don't have the things you want, because you don't pray for them. ³When you pray for things, you don't get them because you want them for the wrong reason—for your own pleasure. *James 4:2–3* GWORD

**CHALLENGE:** Christ has liberated us to be free. Stand firm then and don't submit again to a yoke of slavery. *Galatians 5:1* HCSB

## ℰ❧ FEBRUARY 17 ❦

*Memory Verse 4*

**PROMISE:** And because you belong to him, the power of the life-giving Spirit has freed you from the power of sin that leads to death. *Romans 8:2* NLT

**PRAYER:** Do not remember the iniquities of our forefathers against us; Let Your compassion come quickly to meet us, For we are brought very low. ⁹Help us, O God of our salvation, for the glory of Your name; And deliver us and forgive our sins for Your name's sake. *Psalms 79:8–9* NAS95

**CHALLENGE:** Finally, my brothers and sisters, rejoice in the Lord! To write this again is no trouble to me, and it is a safeguard for you. *Philippians 3:1* NET

## ❧ FEBRUARY 18 ❧

*Memory Verse 4*

**PROMISE:** You save humble people, but your eyes bring down arrogant people. *2 Samuel 22:28* GWORD

**PRAYER:** Some trust in chariots and others in horses, but we depend on the LORD our God. *Psalms 20:7* NET

**CHALLENGE:** Do not be a friend of one who has a bad temper, and never keep company with a hothead, ²⁵or you will learn his ways and set a trap for yourself. *Proverbs 22:24–25* GWORD

## ❧ FEBRUARY 19 ❧

*Memory Verse 4*

**PROMISE:** This is a sure thing: If we die with him, we'll live with him; ¹²If we stick it out with him, we'll rule with him; If we turn our backs on him, he'll turn his back on us; ¹³If we give up on him, he does not give up—for there's no way he can be false to himself. *2 Timothy 2:11–13* MESSAGE

**PRAYER:** But even if I am being poured out like a drink offering on the sacrifice and service of your faith, I am glad and rejoice together with all of you. ¹⁸And in the same way you also should be glad and rejoice together with me. *Philippians 2:17–18* NET

**CHALLENGE:** Set me as a seal on your heart, as a seal on your arm. For love is as strong as death; ardent love is as unrelenting as Sheol. Love's flames are fiery flames—the fiercest of all. *Song 8:6* HCSB

## ❧ FEBRUARY 20 ❧

*Memory Verse 4*

**PROMISE:** Those who control their tongue will have a long life; opening your mouth can ruin everything. *Proverbs 13:3* NLT

**PRAYER:** And I will pray the Father, and He will give you another Helper, that He may abide with you forever—¹⁷the Spirit of truth, whom the world cannot receive, because it neither sees Him nor knows Him; but you know Him, for He dwells with you and will be in you. *John 14:16–17* NKJV

**CHALLENGE:** Oh come, let us worship and bow down; let us kneel before the LORD, our Maker! ⁷For he is our God, and we are the people of his pasture, and the sheep of his hand. *Psalms 95:6–7* ESV

## ℘ FEBRUARY 21 ℘

### *Memory Verse 4*

**PROMISE:** I will not abandon you as orphans, I will come to you. ¹⁹In a little while the world will not see me any longer, but you will see me; because I live, you will live too. *John 14:18–19* NET

**PRAYER:** The LORD is my shepherd, I shall not be in want. ²He makes me lie down in green pastures, he leads me beside quiet waters, ³he restores my soul. He guides me in paths of righteousness for his name's sake. *Psalms 23:1–3* NIV

**CHALLENGE:** Let not sin therefore reign in your mortal body, to make you obey its passions. *Romans 6:12* ESV

## ℘ FEBRUARY 22 ℘

### *Memory Verse 4*

**PROMISE:** He will swallow up death in victory; and the Lord GOD will wipe away tears from off all faces; and the rebuke of his people shall he take away from off all the earth: for the LORD hath spoken it. *Isaiah 25:8* KJV

**PRAYER:** Whenever you stand praying, forgive, if you have anything against anyone, so that your Father who is in heaven will also forgive you your transgressions. *Mark 11:25* NAS95

**CHALLENGE:** Refined speech is not fitting for a godless fool. How much less does lying fit a noble person! Proverbs 17:7 GWORD

## ℰ FEBRUARY 23 ℛ

### *Memory Verse 4*

**PROMISE:** A good reputation is more valuable than costly perfume. And the day you die is better than the day you are born. *Ecclesiastes 7:1* NLT

**PRAYER:** Then will I go to the altar of God, to God, my joy and my delight. I will praise you with the harp, O God, my God. *Psalms 43:4* NIV

**CHALLENGE:** So, then, brothers and sisters, don't let anyone move you off the foundation ‹of your faith›. Always excel in the work you do for the Lord. You know that the hard work you do for the Lord is not pointless. *1 Corinthians 15:58* GWORD

## ℰ FEBRUARY 24 ℛ

### *Memory Verse 4*

**PROMISE:** "And behold, I am coming quickly, and My reward is with Me, to give to every one according to his work. *Revelation 22:12* NKJV

**PRAYER:** When I said, "My feet are slipping," your mercy, O Lord, continued to hold me up. ¹⁹When I worried about many things, your assuring words soothed my soul. *Psalms 94:18–19* GWORD

**CHALLENGE:** Do not plot harm against your neighbor, who lives trustfully near you. ³⁰Do not accuse a man for no reason—when he has done you no harm. *Proverbs 3:29–30* NIV

## ᔙ FEBRUARY 25 ᔗ

*Memory Verse 4*

**PROMISE:** And you will be hated by everyone because of My name. But the one who endures to the end will be delivered. *Mark 13:13* HCSB

**PRAYER:** Your way, O God, is holy; What god is great like our God? ¹⁴You are the God who works wonders; You have made known Your strength among the peoples. *Psalms 77:13–14* NAS95

**CHALLENGE:** So anyone who eats this bread or drinks this cup of the Lord unworthily is guilty of sinning against the body and blood of the Lord. ²⁸That is why you should examine yourself before eating the bread and drinking the cup. ²⁹For if you eat the bread or drink the cup without honoring the body of Christ, you are eating and drinking God's judgment upon yourself. *1 Corinthians 11:27–29* NLT

## ᔙ FEBRUARY 26 ᔗ

*Memory Verse 4*

**PROMISE:** Now he is exalted to the place of highest honor in heaven, at God's right hand. And the Father, as he had promised, gave him the Holy Spirit to pour out upon us, just as you see and hear today. *Acts 2:33* NLT

**PRAYER:** Dear friend, I pray that you may enjoy good health and that all may go well with you, even as your soul is getting along well. *3 John 1:2* NIV

**CHALLENGE:** What good is it, my brothers, if someone says he has faith but does not have works? Can that faith save him? ¹⁵If a brother or sister is poorly clothed and lacking in daily food, ¹⁶and one of you says to them, "Go in peace, be warmed and filled," without giving them the things needed for the body, what good is that? ¹⁷So also faith by itself, if it does not have works, is dead. *James 2:14–17* ESV

## ɞ FEBRUARY 27 ᙗ

*Memory Verse 4*

**PROMISE:** Folly is a joy to him who lacks sense, but a man of understanding walks straight ahead. ²²Without counsel plans fail, but with many advisers they succeed. *Proverbs 15:21–22* ESV

**PRAYER:** The Lord will never desert his people or abandon those who belong to him. *Psalms 94:14* GWORD

**CHALLENGE:** Like newborn babies, crave pure spiritual milk, so that by it you may grow up in your salvation, ³now that you have tasted that the Lord is good. *1 Peter 2:2–3* NIV

## ɞ FEBRUARY 28 ᙗ

*Memory Verse 5*

**PROMISE:** Then I saw a great white throne and One seated on it. Earth and heaven fled from His presence, and no place was found for them. ¹²I also saw the dead, the great and the small, standing before the throne, and books were opened. Another book was opened, which is the book of life, and the dead were judged according to their works by what was written in the books. *Revelation 20:11–12* HCSB

**PRAYER:** O righteous Father! The world has not known You, but I have known You; and these have known that You sent Me. ²⁶And I have declared to them Your name, and will declare it, that the love with which You loved Me may be in them, and I in them." *John 17:25–26* NKJV

**CHALLENGE:** Dear children, let us not love with words or tongue but with actions and in truth. *1 John 3:18* NIV

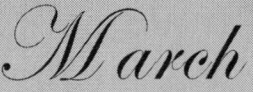

# March

## ℘ MARCH 1 ℘

*Memory Verse 5*

**PROMISE:** When Jesus heard this, He told them, "Those who are well don't need a doctor, but the sick do need one. I didn't come to call the righteous, but sinners." *Mark 2:17* HCSB

**PRAYER:** "I've made myself available to those who haven't bothered to ask. I'm here, ready to be found by those who haven't bothered to look. I kept saying 'I'm here, I'm right here' to a nation that ignored me. ²I reached out day after day to a people who turned their backs on me, People who make wrong turns, who insist on doing things their own way. *Isaiah 65:1–2* MESSAGE

**CHALLENGE:** I am not ashamed of the gospel, because it is the power of God for the salvation of everyone who believes: first for the Jew, then for the Gentile. *Romans 1:16* NIV

## ℘ MARCH 2 ℘

*Memory Verse 5*

**PROMISE:** Love never fails. But where there are prophecies, they will cease; where there are tongues, they will be stilled; where there is knowledge, it will pass away. *1 Corinthians 13:8* NIV

**PRAYER:** How blessed are those who observe his rules, and seek him with all their heart, ³who, moreover, do no wrong, but follow in his footsteps. *Psalms 119:2–3* NET

**CHALLENGE:** Keep my commandments and live, And my teaching as the apple of your eye. ³Bind them on your fingers; Write them on the tablet of your heart. *Proverbs 7:2–3* NAS95

## ᘒ MARCH 3 ᘒ

*Memory Verse 5*

**PROMISE:** Give, and it will be given to you: A good measure, pressed down, shaken together, running over, will be poured into your lap. For the measure you use will be the measure you receive." *Luke 6:38* NET

**PRAYER:** O Lord, let your ear be attentive to the prayer of this your servant and to the prayer of your servants who delight in revering your name. Give your servant success today by granting him favor in the presence of this man." *Nehemiah 1:11* NIV

**CHALLENGE:** Do not be wise in your own eyes; Fear the LORD and turn away from evil. *Proverbs 3:7* NAS95

## ᘒ MARCH 4 ᘒ

*Memory Verse 5*

**PROMISE:** O LORD, who may abide in Your tent? Who may dwell on Your holy hill? ²He who walks with integrity, and works righteousness, And speaks truth in his heart. ³He does not slander with his tongue, Nor does evil to his neighbor, Nor takes up a reproach against his friend; ⁴In whose eyes a reprobate is despised, But who honors those who fear the LORD; He swears to his own hurt and does not change; ⁵He does not put out his money at interest, Nor does he take a bribe against the innocent. He who does these things will never be shaken. *Psalms 15:1–5* NAS95

**PRAYER:** I want men to offer prayers everywhere. They should raise their hands in prayer after putting aside their anger and any quarrels they have with anyone. *1 Timothy 2:8* GWORD

**CHALLENGE:** Know this, my beloved brothers: let every person be quick to hear, slow to speak, slow to anger; ²⁰for the anger of man does not produce the righteousness of God. *James 1:19–20* ESV

## ᔔ MARCH 5 ᔕ

### *Memory Verse 5*

**PROMISE:** Lazy people want much but get little, but those who work hard will prosper. *Proverbs 13:4* NLT

**PRAYER:** I will give you thanks because your deeds are awesome and amazing. You knew me thoroughly; ¹⁵my bones were not hidden from you, when I was made in secret and sewed together in the depths of the earth. ¹⁶Your eyes saw me when I was inside the womb. All the days ordained for me were recorded in your scroll before one of them came into existence. *Psalms 139:14–16* NET

**CHALLENGE:** For through the law I have died to the law, so that I might live for God. I have been crucified with Christ ²⁰and I no longer live, but Christ lives in me. The life I now live in the body, I live by faith in the Son of God, who loved me and gave Himself for me. *Galatians 2:19–20* HCSB

## ᔔ MARCH 6 ᔕ

### *Memory Verse 5*

**PROMISE:** The human mind is the most deceitful of all things. It is incurable. No one can understand how deceitful it is. ¹⁰I, the Lord, search minds and test hearts. I will reward each person for what he has done. I will reward him for the results of his actions. *Jeremiah 17:9–10* GWORD

**PRAYER:** For great is your love, reaching to the heavens; your faithfulness reaches to the skies. *Psalms 57:10* NIV

**CHALLENGE:** "If you love me, you will obey my commandments. *John 14:15* NET

## ഊ MARCH 7 ൧

**PROMISE:** A wicked person will be trapped by his own wrongs, and he will be caught in the ropes of his own sin. ²³He will die for his lack of discipline and stumble around because of his great stupidity. *Proverbs 5:22–23* GWORD

**PRAYER:** Yes, LORD, walking in the way of your laws, we wait for you; your name and renown are the desire of our hearts. *Isaiah 26:8* NIV

**CHALLENGE:** For I have kept the ways of the LORD, And have not wickedly departed from my God. ²²For all His ordinances were before me, And I did not put away His statutes from me. *Psalms 18:21–22* NAS95

## ഊ MARCH 8 ൧

*Memory Verse 5*

**PROMISE:** The one who believes in Me believes not in Me, but in Him who sent Me. ⁴⁵And the one who sees Me sees Him who sent Me. ⁴⁶I have come as a light into the world, so that everyone who believes in Me would not remain in darkness. *John 12:44–46* HCSB

**PRAYER:** My voice rises to God, and I will cry aloud; My voice rises to God, and He will hear me. *Psalms 77:1* NAS95

**CHALLENGE:** So we are no longer to be children, tossed back and forth by waves and carried about by every wind of teaching by the trickery of people who craftily carry out their deceitful schemes. ¹⁵But practicing the truth in love, we will in all things grow up into Christ, who is the head. ¹⁶From him the whole body grows, fitted and held together through every supporting ligament. As each one does its part, the body grows in love. *Ephesians 4:14–16* NET

## ഔ MARCH 9 ൃ

*Memory Verse 5*

**PROMISE:** On the last and most important day of the festival, Jesus stood up and cried out, "If anyone is thirsty, he should come to Me and drink! ³⁸The one who believes in Me, as the Scripture has said, will have streams of living water flow from deep within him." *John 7:37–38* HCSB

**PRAYER:** O LORD, your loyal love fills the earth. Teach me your statutes! *Psalms 119:64* NET

**CHALLENGE:** As the Scripture says, "Anyone who trusts in him will never be put to shame." *Romans 10:11* NIV

## ഔ MARCH 10 ൃ

*Memory Verse 5*

**PROMISE:** O Lord, you are my lamp. The Lord turns my darkness into light. ³⁰With you I can attack a line of soldiers. With my God I can break through barricades. *2 Samuel 22:29–30* GWORD

**PRAYER:** The LORD is far from the wicked, but he hears the prayer of the righteous. *Proverbs 15:29* ESV

**CHALLENGE:** "Then if anyone tells you, 'Look, here is the Messiah,' or 'There he is,' don't believe it. ²²For false messiahs and false prophets will rise up and perform signs and wonders so as to deceive, if possible, even God's chosen ones. ²³Watch out! I have warned you about this ahead of time! *Mark 13:21–23* NLT

## ഔ MARCH 11 ൃ

*Memory Verse 5*

**PROMISE:** The LORD on high is mightier than the noise of many waters, yea, than the mighty waves of the sea. *Psalms 93:4* KJV

**PRAYER:** On return, they beached the boat at Gennesaret. ³⁵When the people got wind that he was back, they sent out word through the neighborhood and rounded up all the sick, ³⁶who asked for permission to touch the edge of his coat. And whoever touched him was healed. *Matthew 14:34–36* MESSAGE

**CHALLENGE:** Whoever has knowledge controls his words, and a person who has understanding is even-tempered. *Proverbs 17:27* GWORD

## ෨ MARCH 12 ൭

*Memory Verse 5*

**PROMISE:** If you keep on biting and devouring each other, watch out or you will be destroyed by each other. *Galatians 5:15* NIV

**PRAYER:** Bless the LORD, O my soul, And forget not all His benefits: ³Who forgives all your iniquities, Who heals all your diseases, ⁴Who redeems your life from destruction, Who crowns you with lovingkindness and tender mercies, ⁵Who satisfies your mouth with good things, So that your youth is renewed like the eagle's. *Psalms 103:2–5* NKJV

**CHALLENGE:** Enjoy what you have rather than desiring what you don't have. Just dreaming about nice things is meaningless—like chasing the wind. *Ecclesiastes 6:9* NLT

## ෨ MARCH 13 ൭

*Memory Verse 5*

**PROMISE:** A soft answer turns away wrath, but a harsh word stirs up anger. *Proverbs 15:1* ESV

**PRAYER:** But now, Lord, you are our Father. We are the clay, and you are our potter. We are the work of your hands. ⁹Don't be too angry, Lord. Don't remember our sin forever. Now look, we are all your people. *Isaiah 64:8–9* GWORD

**CHALLENGE:** For you were bought at a price. Therefore glorify God with your body. *1 Corinthians 6:20* NET

## ✆ MARCH 14 ✆

*Memory Verse 6*

**PROMISE:** Drive out a mocker, and conflict goes too; then quarreling and dishonor will cease. *Proverbs 22:10* HCSB

**PRAYER:** We give thanks to You, O God, we give thanks, For Your name is near; Men declare Your wondrous works. *Psalms 75:1* NAS95

**CHALLENGE:** Respect your mother and father. Observe my days of worship. I am the Lord your God. *Leviticus 19:3* GWORD

## ✆ MARCH 15 ✆

*Memory Verse 6*

**PROMISE:** The life of the godly is full of light and joy, but the light of the wicked will be snuffed out. *Proverbs 13:9* NLT

**PRAYER:** Praise the LORD! Praise God in his sanctuary; praise him in his mighty heavens! ²Praise him for his mighty deeds; praise him according to his excellent greatness! *Psalms 150:1–2* ESV

**CHALLENGE:** Dear friends, I urge you, as aliens and strangers in the world, to abstain from sinful desires, which war against your soul. ¹²Live such good lives among the pagans that, though they accuse you of doing wrong, they may see your good deeds and glorify God on the day he visits us. *1 Peter 2:11–12* NIV

## ᔥ MARCH **16** ᘇ

*Memory Verse 6*

**PROMISE:** Because of the LORD's faithful love we do not perish, for His mercies never end. They are new every morning; great is Your faithfulness!a *Lamentations 3:22–23* HCSB

**PRAYER:** In the middle of the night I arise to thank you for your just regulations. ⁶³I am a friend to all your loyal followers, and to those who keep your precepts. *Psalms 119:62–63* NET

**CHALLENGE:** Give to the one who asks you, and do not turn away from the one who wants to borrow from you. *Matthew 5:42* NIV

## ᔥ MARCH **17** ᘇ

*Memory Verse 6*

**PROMISE:** Grandchildren are the crown of grandparents, and parents are the glory of their children. *Proverbs 17:6* GWORD

**PRAYER:** For great is the LORD, and greatly to be praised; he is to be feared above all gods. ⁵For all the gods of the peoples are worthless idols, but the LORD made the heavens. ⁶Splendor and majesty are before him; strength and beauty are in his sanctuary. *Psalms 96:4–6* ESV

**CHALLENGE:** For our light and momentary troubles are achieving for us an eternal glory that far outweighs them all. ¹⁸So we fix our eyes not on what is seen, but on what is unseen. For what is seen is temporary, but what is unseen is eternal. *2 Corinthians 4:17–18* NIV

## ᔥ MARCH **18** ᘇ

*Memory Verse 6*

**PROMISE:** The Lord will rescue me from every evil deed, and will bring me safely to His heavenly kingdom; to Him be the glory forever and ever. Amen. *2 Timothy 4:18* NAS95

**PRAYER:** I confess the sins we Israelites, including myself and my father's house, have committed against you. ⁷We have acted very wickedly toward you. We have not obeyed the commands, decrees and laws you gave your servant Moses. *Nehemiah 1:6–7* NIV

**CHALLENGE:** Instead of being motivated by selfish ambition or vanity, each of you should, in humility, be moved to treat one another as more important than yourself. ⁴Each of you should be concerned not only about your own interests, but about the interests of others as well. *Philippians 2:3–4* NET

## ᔕᒧ MARCH 19 ᥴᔕ

*Memory Verse 6*

**PROMISE:** But Christ has indeed been raised from the dead, the firstfruits of those who have fallen asleep. ²¹For since death came through a man, the resurrection of the dead comes also through a man. ²²For as in Adam all die, so in Christ all will be made alive. *1 Corinthians 15:20–22* NIV

**PRAYER:** Give to the Lord, you families of the nations. Give to the Lord glory and power. ²⁹Give to the Lord the glory his name deserves. Bring an offering, and come to him. Worship the Lord in ‹his› holy splendor. *1 Chronicles 16:28–29* GWORD

**CHALLENGE:** When they persisted in questioning Him, He stood up and said to them, "The one without sin among you should be the first to throw a stone at her." *John 8:7* HCSB

## ᔕᒧ MARCH 20 ᥴᔕ

*Memory Verse 6*

**PROMISE:** And he said unto them, The sabbath was made for man, and not man for the sabbath: ²⁸Therefore the Son of man is Lord also of the sabbath. *Mark 2:27–28* KJV

**PRAYER:** Martha then said to Jesus, "Lord, if You had been here, my brother would not have died. [22]"Even now I know that whatever You ask of God, God will give You." *John 11:21–22* NAS95

**CHALLENGE:** So we must not get tired of doing good, for we will reap at the proper time if we don't give up. *Galatians 6:9* HCSB

## MARCH 21

*Memory Verse 6*

**PROMISE:** For wisdom is better than rubies, And all the things one may desire cannot be compared with her. [12]"I, wisdom, dwell with prudence, And find out knowledge and discretion. *Proverbs 8:11–12* NKJV

**PRAYER:** O LORD God of hosts, who is mighty as you are, O LORD, with your faithfulness all around you? [9]You rule the raging of the sea; when its waves rise, you still them. *Psalms 89:8–9* ESV

**CHALLENGE:** "You are the light of the world. A city on a hill cannot be hidden. [15]Neither do people light a lamp and put it under a bowl. Instead they put it on its stand, and it gives light to everyone in the house. [16]In the same way, let your light shine before men, that they may see your good deeds and praise your Father in heaven. *Matthew 5:14–16* NIV

## MARCH 22

*Memory Verse 6*

**PROMISE:** The rich rule over the poor, and the borrower is a slave to the lender. *Proverbs 22:7* HCSB

**PRAYER:** Preserve me, O God, for I take refuge in You. [2]I said to the LORD, "You are my Lord; I have no good besides You." *Psalms 16:1–2* NAS95

**CHALLENGE:** But you, dear friends, must build each other up in your most holy faith, pray in the power of the Holy Spirit, [21]and await the mercy of our Lord Jesus Christ, who will bring you eternal life. In this way, you will keep yourselves safe in God's love. *Jude 1:20–21* NLT

## ✂ MARCH 23 ✄

### *Memory Verse 6*

**PROMISE:** I am the Alpha and the Omega, the Beginning and the End, the First and the Last." *Revelation 22:13* NKJV

**PRAYER:** Thank God that he gives us the victory through our Lord Jesus Christ. *1 Corinthians 15:57* GWORD

**CHALLENGE:** Wise people think before they act; fools don't—and even brag about their foolishness. *Proverbs 13:16* NLT

## ✂ MARCH 24 ✄

### *Memory Verse 6*

**PROMISE:** "But in those days, after that tribulation: The sun will be darkened, and the moon will not shed its light; ²⁵the stars will be falling from the sky, and the celestial powers will be shaken. ²⁶Then they will see the Son of Man coming in clouds with great power and glory. ²⁷He will send out the angels and gather His elect from the four winds, from the end of the earth to the end of the sky. *Mark 13:24–27* HCSB

**PRAYER:** O Lord, the Hope of Israel, all who abandon you will be put to shame. Those who turn away from you will be written in dust, because they abandon the Lord, the fountain of life-giving water. *Jeremiah 17:13* GWORD

**CHALLENGE:** For in the gospel a righteousness from God is revealed, a righteousness that is by faith from first to last, just as it is written: "The righteous will live by faith." *Romans 1:17* NIV

## ⁊ MARCH 25 ☯

*Memory Verse 6*

**PROMISE:** As iron sharpens iron, so one man sharpens another. *Proverbs 27:17* NIV

**PRAYER:** He said to his disciples, "The harvest is great, but the workers are few. ³⁸So pray to the Lord who is in charge of the harvest; ask him to send more workers into his fields." *Matthew 9:37–38* NLT

**CHALLENGE:** For all people walk each in the name of his god, But we will walk in the name of the LORD our God Forever and ever. *Micah 4:5* NKJV

## ⁊ MARCH 26 ☯

*Memory Verse 6*

**PROMISE:** "I tell you the solemn truth, the one who hears my message and believes the one who sent me has eternal life and will not be condemned, but has crossed over from death to life. *John 5:24* NET

**PRAYER:** Yours is the day, Yours also is the night; You have prepared the light and the sun. ¹⁷You have established all the boundaries of the earth; You have made summer and winter. *Psalms 74:16–17* NAS95

**CHALLENGE:** Don't you know that the runners in a stadium all race, but only one receives the prize? Run in such a way to win the prize. *1 Corinthians 9:24* HCSB

## ⁊ MARCH 27 ☯

*Memory Verse 6*

**PROMISE:** For those who live according to the flesh set their minds on the things of the flesh, but those who live according to the Spirit set their minds on the things of the Spirit. ⁶For to set the mind on the flesh is death, but to set the mind on the Spirit is life and peace. *Romans 8:5–6* ESV

**PRAYER:** Even when I must walk through the darkest valley, I fear no danger, for you are with me; your rod and your staff reassure me. *Psalms 23:4* NET

**CHALLENGE:** He who is slow to anger is better than the mighty, And he who rules his spirit, than he who captures a city. *Proverbs 16:32* NAS95

## ഌ MARCH 28 ☙

*Memory Verse 7*

**PROMISE:** Now the LORD has fulfilled his promise that he made. For I have risen in the place of David my father, and sit on the throne of Israel, as the LORD promised, and I have built the house for the name of the LORD, the God of Israel. *1 Kings 8:20* ESV

**PRAYER:** But the fruit of the Spirit is love, joy, peace, patience, kindness, goodness, faithfulness, [23]gentleness, and self-control. Against such things there is no law. *Galatians 5:22–23* NET

**CHALLENGE:** Do not fret because of evil men or be envious of the wicked, [20]for the evil man has no future hope, and the lamp of the wicked will be snuffed out. *Proverbs 24:19–20* NIV

## ഌ MARCH 29 ☙

*Memory Verse 7*

**PROMISE:** There is one God. There is also one mediator between God and humans—a human, Christ Jesus. [6]He sacrificed himself for all people to free them from their sins. This message is valid for every era. *1 Timothy 2:5–6* GWORD

**PRAYER:** And he entered the temple and began to drive out those who sold, [46]saying to them, "It is written, 'My house shall be a house of prayer,' but you have made it a den of robbers." *Luke 19:45–46* ESV

**CHALLENGE:** I did not at all mean with the immoral people of this world, or with the covetous and swindlers, or with idolaters, for then you would have to go out of the world. ¹¹But actually, I wrote to you not to associate with any so-called brother if he is an immoral person, or covetous, or an idolater, or a reviler, or a drunkard, or a swindler—not even to eat with such a one. *1 Corinthians 5:10–11* NAS95

## ॐ MARCH 30 ॐ

*Memory Verse 7*

**PROMISE:** Your servant has killed both lion and bear; and this uncircumcised Philistine will be like one of them, seeing he has defied the armies of the living God." ³⁷Moreover David said, "The LORD, who delivered me from the paw of the lion and from the paw of the bear, He will deliver me from the hand of this Philistine." And Saul said to David, "Go, and the LORD be with you!" *1 Samuel 17:36–37* NKJV

**PRAYER:** My heart is steadfast, O God, my heart is steadfast; I will sing and make music. ⁸Awake, my soul! Awake, harp and lyre! I will awaken the dawn. ⁹I will praise you, O Lord, among the nations; I will sing of you among the peoples. *Psalms 57:7–9* NIV

**CHALLENGE:** Do everything without grumbling or arguing, ¹⁵so that you may be blameless and pure, children of God without blemish though you live in a crooked and perverse society, in which you shine as lights in the world *Philippians 2:14–16* NET

## ॐ MARCH 31 ॐ

*Memory Verse 7*

**PROMISE:** The LORD is my source of security. I have determined to follow your instructions. ⁵⁸I seek your favor with all my heart. Have mercy on me as you promised! *Psalms 119:57–58* NET

**PRAYER:** My soul yearns for you in the night; in the morning my spirit longs for you. When your judgments come upon the earth, the people of the world learn righteousness. *Isaiah 26:9* NIV

**CHALLENGE:** So speak and so act as those who are to be judged under the law of liberty. [13]For judgment is without mercy to one who has shown no mercy. Mercy triumphs over judgment. *James 2:12–13* ESV

# April

## ᔈ APRIL 1 ᔑ

*Memory Verse 7*

**PROMISE:** The LORD is merciful and gracious, Slow to anger, and abounding in mercy. *Psalms 103:8* NKJV

**PRAYER:** Father, I desire that they also, whom you have given me, may be with me where I am, to see my glory that you have given me because you loved me before the foundation of the world. *John 17:24* ESV

**CHALLENGE:** Summoning the crowd along with His disciples, He said to them, "If anyone wants to be My follower, he must deny himself, take up his cross, and follow Me. ³⁵For whoever wants to save his life will lose it, but whoever loses his life because of Me and the gospel will save it. ³⁶For what does it benefit a man to gain the whole world yet lose his life? *Mark 8:34–36* HCSB

## ᔈ APRIL 2 ᔑ

*Memory Verse 7*

**PROMISE:** God's way is perfect! The promise of the Lord has proven to be true. He is a shield to all those who take refuge in him. *2 Samuel 22:31* GWORD

**PRAYER:** But now thus says the LORD, he who created you, O Jacob, he who formed you, O Israel: "Fear not, for I have redeemed you; I have called you by name, you are mine. *Isaiah 43:1* ESV

**CHALLENGE:** For am I now trying to win the favor of people, or God? Or am I striving to please people? If I were still trying to please people, I would not be a slave of Christ. *Galatians 1:10* HCSB

## ᔓ APRIL 3 ᕰ

### *Memory Verse 7*

**PROMISE:** If you ignore criticism, you will end in poverty and disgrace; if you accept correction, you will be honored. *Proverbs 13:18* NLT

**PRAYER:** For, behold, those who are far from You will perish; You have destroyed all those who are unfaithful to You. ²⁸But as for me, the nearness of God is my good; I have made the Lord GOD my refuge, That I may tell of all Your works. *Psalms 73:27–28* NAS95

**CHALLENGE:** Don't let yourselves get taken in by religious smooth talk. God gets furious with people who are full of religious sales talk but want nothing to do with him. ⁷Don't even hang around people like that. *Ephesians 5:6–7* MESSAGE

## ᔓ APRIL 4 ᕰ

### *Memory Verse 7*

**PROMISE:** Fear-of-GOD is a school in skilled living—first you learn humility, then you experience glory. *Proverbs 15:33* MESSAGE

**PRAYER:** You demand that your precepts be carefully kept. ⁵If only I were predisposed to keep your statutes! ⁶Then I would not be ashamed, if I were focused on all your commands. *Psalms 119:4–6* NET

**CHALLENGE:** So when you give to the needy, do not announce it with trumpets, as the hypocrites do in the synagogues and on the streets, to be honored by men. I tell you the truth, they have received their reward in full. ³But when you give to the needy, do not let your left hand know what your right hand is doing, ⁴so that your giving may be in secret. Then your Father, who sees what is done in secret, will reward you. *Matthew 6:2–4* NIV

## ❧ APRIL 5 ☙

*Memory Verse 7*

**PROMISE:** The fear of the LORD is hatred of evil. Pride and arrogance and the way of evil and perverted speech I hate. *Proverbs 8:13* ESV

**PRAYER:** Now may God our Father himself and our Lord Jesus direct our way to you. ¹²And may the Lord cause you to increase and abound in love for one another and for all, just as we do for you, ¹³so that your hearts are strengthened in holiness to be blameless before our God and Father at the coming of our Lord Jesus with all his saints. *1 Thessalonians 3:11–13* NET

**CHALLENGE:** It was for the sake of the Name that they went out, receiving no help from the pagans. ⁸We ought therefore to show hospitality to such men so that we may work together for the truth. *3 John 1:7–8* NIV

## ❧ APRIL 6 ☙

*Memory Verse 7*

**PROMISE:** Or do you have contempt for the wealth of his kindness, forbearance, and patience, and yet do not know that God's kindness leads you to repentance? *Romans 2:4* NET

**PRAYER:** "O LORD, God of heaven, the great and awesome God, who keeps his covenant of love with those who love him and obey his commands, ⁶let your ear be attentive and your eyes open to hear the prayer your servant is praying before you day and night for your servants, the people of Israel. *Nehemiah 1:5–6* NIV

**CHALLENGE:** "You don't have enough faith," Jesus told them. "I tell you the truth, if you had faith even as small as a mustard seed, you could say to this mountain, 'Move from here to there,' and it would move. Nothing would be impossible." *Matthew 17:20* NLT

## ℘ APRIL 7 ℘

*Memory Verse 7*

**PROMISE:** Thanks be to the Lord! He has given his people Israel rest, as he had promised. None of the good promises he made through his servant Moses has failed to come true. *1 Kings 8:56* GWORD

**PRAYER:** With all my heart I seek you. Do not allow me to stray from your commands! *Psalms 119:10* NET

**CHALLENGE:** They sold their property and possessions and shared the money with those in need. ⁴⁶They worshiped together at the Temple each day, met in homes for the Lord's Supper, and shared their meals with great joy and generosity—⁴⁷all the while praising God and enjoying the goodwill of all the people. And each day the Lord added to their fellowship those who were being saved. *Acts 2:45–47* NLT

## ℘ APRIL 8 ℘

*Memory Verse 7*

**PROMISE:** He who covers his sins will not prosper, But whoever confesses and forsakes them will have mercy. *Proverbs 28:13* NKJV

**PRAYER:** But because Jesus lives forever, his priesthood lasts forever. ²⁵Therefore he is able, once and forever, to save those who come to God through him. He lives forever to intercede with God on their behalf. *Hebrews 7:24–25* NLT

**CHALLENGE:** To the present hour we are hungry and thirsty, poorly clothed, brutally treated, and without a roof over our heads. ¹²We do hard work, toiling with our own hands. When we are verbally abused, we respond with a blessing, when persecuted, we endure, ¹³when people lie about us, we answer in a friendly manner. We are the world's dirt and scum, even now. *1 Corinthians 4:11–13* NET

## ∞ APRIL **9** ∞

*Memory Verse 7*

**PROMISE:** "Do not judge, and you will not be judged; do not condemn, and you will not be condemned; forgive, and you will be forgiven. *Luke 6:37* NET

**PRAYER:** Know that the LORD has set apart the godly for himself; the LORD will hear when I call to him. *Psalms 4:3* NIV

**CHALLENGE:** "Now concerning that day or hour no one knows—neither the angels in heaven nor the Son—except the Father. ³³Watch! Be alert! For you don't know when the time is coming. *Mark 13:32–33* HCSB

## ∞ APRIL **10** ∞

*Memory Verse 7*

**PROMISE:** Come close to God, and he will come close to you. Clean up your lives, you sinners, and clear your minds, you doubters. *James 4:8* GWORD

**PRAYER:** The glory that you have given me I have given to them, that they may be one even as we are one, ²³I in them and you in me, that they may become perfectly one, so that the world may know that you sent me and loved them even as you loved me. *John 17:22–24* ESV

**CHALLENGE:** Do not envy a violent man or choose any of his ways, ³²for the LORD detests a perverse man but takes the upright into his confidence. *Proverbs 3:31–32* NIV

## ∞ APRIL **11** ∞

*Memory Verse 8*

**PROMISE:** For the mind that is set on the flesh is hostile to God, for it does not submit to God's law; indeed, it cannot. ⁸Those who are in the flesh cannot please God. ⁹You, however, are not in the flesh but in the Spirit, if in fact the Spirit of God dwells in you. Anyone who does not have the Spirit of Christ does not belong to him. ¹⁰But if Christ is in you, although the body is dead because of sin, the Spirit is life because of righteousness. *Romans 8:7–10* ESV

**PRAYER:** We pray earnestly night and day to see you in person and make up what may be lacking in your faith. *1 Thessalonians 3:10* NET

**CHALLENGE:** As we have therefore opportunity, let us do good unto all men, especially unto them who are of the household of faith. *Galatians 6:10* KJV

## ℘ APRIL 12 ℃

*Memory Verse 8*

**PROMISE:** Therefore say to them: This is what the Lord GOD says: None of My words will be delayed any longer. The message I speak will be fulfilled." This is the declaration of the Lord GOD. *Ezekiel 12:28* HCSB

**PRAYER:** I will lift my hands to your commands, which I love, and I will meditate on your statutes. *Psalms 119:48* NET

**CHALLENGE:** My child, don't go along with them! Stay far away from their paths. ¹⁶They rush to commit evil deeds. They hurry to commit murder. ¹⁷If a bird sees a trap being set, it knows to stay away. *Proverbs 1:15–17* NLT

## ℘ APRIL 13 ℃

*Memory Verse 8*

**PROMISE:** There is another serious problem I have seen under the sun. Hoarding riches harms the saver. ¹⁴Money is put into risky investments that turn sour, and everything is lost. In the end, there is nothing left to pass on to one's children. ¹⁵We all come to the end of our lives as naked and empty-handed as on the day we were born. We can't take our riches with us. *Ecclesiastes 5:13–15* NLT

**PRAYER:** For who is God, except the LORD? And who is a rock, except our God? *2 Samuel 22:32* NKJV

**CHALLENGE:** He who gives attention to the word will find good, And blessed is he who trusts in the LORD. *Proverbs 16:20* NAS95

## ෨ APRIL **14** ୯ର

### *Memory Verse 8*

**PROMISE:** When you pass through the waters, I will be with you; and through the rivers, they shall not overwhelm you; when you walk through fire you shall not be burned, and the flame shall not consume you. *Isaiah 43:2* ESV

**PRAYER:** Hear a just cause, O LORD, give heed to my cry; Give ear to my prayer, which is not from deceitful lips. *Psalms 17:1* NAS95

**CHALLENGE:** "You have heard that it was said, 'Love your neighbor and hate your enemy.' 44But I tell you: Love your enemies and pray for those who persecute you, 45that you may be sons of your Father in heaven. He causes his sun to rise on the evil and the good, and sends rain on the righteous and the unrighteous. 46If you love those who love you, what reward will you get? Are not even the tax collectors doing that? *Matthew 5:43–46* NIV

## ෨ APRIL **15** ୯ର

### *Memory Verse 8*

**PROMISE:** Good will come to him who is generous and lends freely, who conducts his affairs with justice. 6Surely he will never be shaken; a righteous man will be remembered forever. *Psalms 112:5–6* NIV

**PRAYER:** "I do not ask for these only, but also for those who will believe in me through their word, 21that they may all be one, just as you, Father, are in me, and I in you, that they also may be in us, so that the world may believe that you have sent me. *John 17:20–21* ESV

**CHALLENGE:** Do not extinguish the Spirit. ²⁰Do not treat prophecies with contempt. ²¹But examine all things; hold fast to what is good. ²²Stay away from every form of evil. *1 Thessalonians 5:19–22* NET

## ❧ APRIL 16 ☙

*Memory Verse 8*

**PROMISE:** God arms me with strength and makes my way perfect. ³³He makes my feet like those of a deer and gives me sure footing on high places. *Psalms 18:32–33* GWORD

**PRAYER:** Can you fathom the depths of God or discover the limits of the Almighty? ⁸They are higher than the heavens—what can you do? They are deeper than Sheol—what can you know? ⁹Their measure is longer than the earth and wider than the sea. *Job 11:7–9* HCSB

**CHALLENGE:** Walk with the wise and become wise; associate with fools and get in trouble. ²¹Trouble chases sinners, while blessings reward the righteous. *Proverbs 13:20–21* NLT

## ❧ APRIL 17 ☙

*Memory Verse 8*

**PROMISE:** Strengthen the feeble hands, steady the knees that give way; ⁴say to those with fearful hearts, "Be strong, do not fear; your God will come, he will come with vengeance; with divine retribution he will come to save you." *Isaiah 35:3–4* NIV

**PRAYER:** Therefore, if there is any encouragement in Christ, any comfort provided by love, any fellowship in the Spirit, any affection or mercy, ²complete my joy and be of the same mind, by having the same love, being united in spirit, and having one purpose. *Philippians 2:1–2* NET

**CHALLENGE:** Mark a life of discipline and live wisely; don't squander your precious life. *Proverbs 8:33* MESSAGE

## ❧ APRIL **18** ☙

*Memory Verse 8*

**PROMISE:** Then I heard a loud voice shouting across the heavens, "It has come at last—salvation and power and the Kingdom of our God, and the authority of his Christ. For the accuser of our brothers and sisters has been thrown down to earth—the one who accuses them before our God day and night. ¹¹And they have defeated him by the blood of the Lamb and by their testimony. And they did not love their lives so much that they were afraid to die. *Revelation 12:10–11* NLT

**PRAYER:** LORD, you establish peace for us; all that we have accomplished you have done for us. *Isaiah 26:12* NIV

**CHALLENGE:** I will be secure, for I seek your precepts. ⁴⁶I will speak about your regulations before kings and not be ashamed. ⁴⁷I will find delight in your commands, which I love. *Psalms 119:45–47* NET

## ❧ APRIL **19** ☙

*Memory Verse 8*

**PROMISE:** The one who calls you is faithful and he will do it. *1 Thessalonians 5:24* NIV

**PRAYER:** Now to the King eternal, immortal, invisible, the only God, be honor and glory forever and ever. Amen. *1 Timothy 1:17* HCSB

**CHALLENGE:** Those who spare the rod of discipline hate their children. Those who love their children care enough to discipline them. *Proverbs 13:24* NLT

## &) APRIL **20** &

*Memory Verse 8*

**PROMISE:** And I will do whatever you ask in my name, so that the Father may be glorified in the Son. ¹⁴If you ask me anything in my name, I will do it. *John 14:13–14* NET

**PRAYER:** Be exalted, O God, above the heavens; let your glory be over all the earth. *Psalms 57:5* NIV

**CHALLENGE:** We should live decently, as people who live in the light of day. Wild parties, drunkenness, sexual immorality, promiscuity, rivalry, and jealousy cannot be part of our lives. ¹⁴Instead, live like the Lord Jesus Christ did, and forget about satisfying the desires of your sinful nature. *Romans 13:13–14* GWORD

## &) APRIL **21** &

*Memory Verse 8*

**PROMISE:** "At the time of those kings, the God of heaven will establish a kingdom that will never be destroyed. No other people will be permitted to rule it. It will smash all the other kingdoms and put an end to them. But it will be established forever. *Daniel 2:44* GWORD

**PRAYER:** And now these three remain: faith, hope and love. But the greatest of these is love. *1 Corinthians 13:13* NIV

**CHALLENGE:** This is how we know what love is: Jesus Christ laid down his life for us. And we ought to lay down our lives for our brothers. *1 John 3:16* NIV

## &) APRIL **22** &

*Memory Verse 8*

**PROMISE:** For a time is coming when people will no longer listen to sound and wholesome teaching. They will follow their own desires and will look for teachers who will tell them whatever their itching ears want to hear. ⁴They will reject the truth and chase after myths. *2 Timothy 4:3–4* NLT

**PRAYER:** Then Moses and the Israelites sang this song to the LORD. They said: I will sing to the LORD, for He is highly exalted; He has thrown the horse and its rider into the sea. ²The LORD is my strength and my song; He has become my salvation. This is my God, and I will praise Him, my father's God, and I will exalt Him. ³The LORD is a warrior; Yahweh is His name. *Exodus 15:1–3* HCSB

**CHALLENGE:** Do not gloat when your enemy falls; when he stumbles, do not let your heart rejoice, ¹⁸or the LORD will see and disapprove and turn his wrath away from him. *Proverbs 24:17–18* NIV

## ಌ APRIL 23 ಬ

*Memory Verse 8*

**PROMISE:** Love is patient, love is kind. It does not envy, it does not boast, it is not proud. ⁵It is not rude, it is not self-seeking, it is not easily angered, it keeps no record of wrongs. ⁶Love does not delight in evil but rejoices with the truth. ⁷It always protects, always trusts, always hopes, always perseveres. *1 Corinthians 13:4–7* NIV

**PRAYER:** They are not of the world, just as I am not of the world. ¹⁷Sanctify them in the truth; your word is truth. ¹⁸As you sent me into the world, so I have sent them into the world. ¹⁹And for their sake I consecrate myself, that they also may be sanctified in truth. *John 17:16–19* ESV

**CHALLENGE:** Therefore, having laid aside falsehood, each one of you speak the truth with his neighbor, for we are members of one another. *Ephesians 4:25* NET

## ❧ APRIL 24 ❧

*Memory Verse 8*

**PROMISE:** Does the Spirit of the one who brought Jesus back to life live in you? Then the one who brought Christ back to life will also make your mortal bodies alive by his Spirit who lives in you. *Romans 8:11* GWORD

**PRAYER:** Ask of me, and I will make the nations your inheritance, the ends of the earth your possession. *Psalms 2:8* NIV

**CHALLENGE:** If we are thrown into the blazing furnace, the God whom we serve is able to save us. He will rescue us from your power, Your Majesty. ¹⁸But even if he doesn't, we want to make it clear to you, Your Majesty, that we will never serve your gods or worship the gold statue you have set up." *Daniel 3:17–18* NLT

## ❧ APRIL 25 ❧

*Memory Verse 9*

**PROMISE:** When the LORD rises to shake the earth, his enemies will crawl into holes in the ground. They will hide in caves in the rocks from the terror of the LORD and the glory of his majesty. *Isaiah 2:19* NLT

**PRAYER:** In you, O LORD, I have taken refuge; let me never be put to shame; deliver me in your righteousness. *Psalms 31:1* NIV

**CHALLENGE:** ⁸"Remember the Sabbath day by keeping it holy. ⁹Six days you shall labor and do all your work, ¹⁰but the seventh day is a Sabbath to the LORD your God. On it you shall not do any work, neither you, nor your son or daughter, nor your manservant or maid-servant, nor your animals, nor the alien within your gates. ¹¹For in six days the LORD made the heavens and the earth, the sea, and all that is in them, but he rested on the seventh day. Therefore the LORD blessed the Sabbath day and made it holy. *Exodus 20:7–11* NIV

## ∽ APRIL 26 ∾

*Memory Verse 9*

**PROMISE:** I will transform the battered into a company of the elite. I will make a strong nation out of the long lost, A showcase exhibit of GOD's rule in action, as I rule from Mount Zion, from here to eternity. *Micah 4:7* MESSAGE

**PRAYER:** In the shelter of your presence you hide them from the intrigues of men; in your dwelling you keep them safe from accusing tongues. ²¹Praise be to the LORD, for he showed his wonderful love to me when I was in a besieged city. *Psalms 31:20–21* NIV

**CHALLENGE:** Train up a child in the way he should go, And when he is old he will not depart from it. *Proverbs 22:6* NKJV

## ∽ APRIL 27 ∾

*Memory Verse 9*

**PROMISE:** Let your blessings reach me, O Lord. Save me as you promised. *Psalms 119:41* GWORD

**PRAYER:** When I heard these things, I sat down and wept. For some days I mourned and fasted and prayed before the God of heaven. *Nehemiah 1:4* NIV

**CHALLENGE:** We live by faith, not by sight. ⁸We are confident, I say, and would prefer to be away from the body and at home with the Lord. ⁹So we make it our goal to please him, whether we are at home in the body or away from it. ¹⁰For we must all appear before the judgment seat of Christ, that each one may receive what is due him for the things done while in the body, whether good or bad. *2 Corinthians 5:7–10* NIV

## ❧ APRIL 28 ☙

*Memory Verse 9*

**PROMISE:** If you remain in me and my words remain in you, ask whatever you want, and it will be done for you. ⁸My Father is honored by this, that you bear much fruit and show that you are my disciples. *John 15:7–8* NET

**PRAYER:** Then the king said to the man of God, "Intercede with the LORD your God and pray for me that my hand may be restored." So the man of God interceded with the LORD, and the king's hand was restored and became as it was before. *1 Kings 13:6* NIV

**CHALLENGE:** Do not testify against your neighbor without cause, or use your lips to deceive. ²⁹Do not say, "I'll do to him as he has done to me; I'll pay that man back for what he did." *Proverbs 24:28–29* NIV

## ❧ APRIL 29 ☙

*Memory Verse 9*

**PROMISE:** Owe no one anything except to love one another, for he who loves another has fulfilled the law. *Romans 13:8* NKJV

**PRAYER:** As the deer pants for streams of water, so my soul pants for you, O God. ²My soul thirsts for God, for the living God. When can I go and meet with God? *Psalms 42:1–2* NIV

**CHALLENGE:** For you were called to freedom, brothers and sisters; only do not use your freedom as an opportunity to indulge your flesh, but through love serve one another. ¹⁴For the whole law can be summed up in a single commandment, namely, "You must love your neighbor as yourself." *Galatians 5:13–15* NET

# ℰꙨ APRIL **30** ℭ℟

*Memory Verse 9*

**PROMISE:** Flood waters can't drown love, torrents of rain can't put it out. Love can't be bought, love can't be sold—it's not to be found in the marketplace. *Song 8:7* MESSAGE

**PRAYER:** Grace to you and peace from God our Father and the Lord Jesus Christ, ⁴who gave Himself for our sins so that He might rescue us from this present evil age, according to the will of our God and Father, ⁵to whom be the glory forevermore. Amen. *Galatians 1:3–5* NAS95

**CHALLENGE:** Trust in him at all times, you people! Pour out your hearts before him! God is our shelter! *Psalms 62:8* NET

## ❧ MAY 1 ☙

*Memory Verse 9*

**PROMISE:** God "will give to each person according to what he has done." ⁷To those who by persistence in doing good seek glory, honor and immortality, he will give eternal life. ⁸But for those who are self-seeking and who reject the truth and follow evil, there will be wrath and anger. *Romans 2:6–8* NIV

**PRAYER:** Then King David went in and sat before the LORD; and he said: "Who am I, O Lord GOD? And what is my house, that You have brought me this far? *2 Samuel 7:18* NKJV

**CHALLENGE:** But as for me, I will never boast about anything except the cross of our Lord Jesus Christ. The world has been crucified to me through the cross, and I to the world. *Galatians 6:14–15* HCSB

## ❧ MAY 2 ☙

*Memory Verse 9*

**PROMISE:** Far better to be right and poor than to be wrong and rich. *Proverbs 16:8* MESSAGE

**PRAYER:** Look, I long for your precepts. Revive me with your deliverance! ⁴¹(Vav) May I experience your loyal love, O LORD, and your deliverance, as you promised. *Psalms 119:40–41* NET

**CHALLENGE:** Let the peace of Christ rule in your hearts, since as members of one body you were called to peace. And be thankful. ¹⁶Let the word of Christ dwell in you richly as you teach and admonish one another with all wisdom, and as you sing psalms, hymns and spiritual songs with gratitude in your hearts to God. [17]And whatever you do, whether in word or deed, do it all in the name of the Lord Jesus, giving thanks to God the Father through him. *Colossians 3:15–17* NIV

## ෨ MAY 3 ඥ

*Memory Verse 9*

**PROMISE:** So an elder must be a man whose life is above reproach. He must be faithful to his wife. He must exercise self-control, live wisely, and have a good reputation. He must enjoy having guests in his home, and he must be able to teach. [3]He must not be a heavy drinker or be violent. He must be gentle, not quarrelsome, and not love money. [4]He must manage his own family well, having children who respect and obey him. *1 Timothy 3:2–4* NLT

**PRAYER:** Whom have I in heaven but You? And besides You, I desire nothing on earth. [26]My flesh and my heart may fail, But God is the strength of my heart and my portion forever. *Psalms 73:25–26* NAS95

**CHALLENGE:** Do not swerve to the right or the left; keep your foot from evil. *Proverbs 4:27* NIV

## ෨ MAY 4 ඥ

*Memory Verse 9*

**PROMISE:** For we are His workmanship, created in Christ Jesus for good works, which God prepared beforehand so that we would walk in them. *Ephesians 2:10* NAS95

**PRAYER:** While I was with them, I kept them in your name, which you have given me. I have guarded them, and not one of them has been lost except the son of destruction, that the Scripture might be fulfilled. [13]But now I am coming to you, and these things I speak in the world, that they may have my joy fulfilled in themselves. [14]I have given them your word, and the world has hated them because they are not of the world, just as I am not of the world. ¹⁵I do not ask that you take them out of the world, but that you keep them from the evil one. *John 17:12–15* ESV

**CHALLENGE:** Who is God but the Lord? Who is a rock except our God? *Psalms 18:31* GWORD

## ℰᏒ MAY 5 ᏒᎧ

### *Memory Verse 9*

**PROMISE:** Everyone must submit to governing authorities. For all authority comes from God, and those in positions of authority have been placed there by God. ²So anyone who rebels against authority is rebelling against what God has instituted, and they will be punished. *Romans 13:1–2* NLT

**PRAYER:** You prepare a table before me in the presence of my enemies. You anoint my head with oil; my cup overflows. ⁶Surely goodness and love will follow me all the days of my life, and I will dwell in the house of the LORD forever. *Psalms 23:5–6* NIV

**CHALLENGE:** He said to them, "Go into all the world and preach the good news to all creation. *Mark 16:15* NIV

## ℰᏒ MAY 6 ᏒᎧ

### *Memory Verse 9*

**PROMISE:** The fear of the LORD is the beginning of wisdom, And the knowledge of the Holy One is understanding. ¹¹For by me your days will be multiplied, And years of life will be added to you. ¹²If you are wise, you are wise for yourself, And if you scoff, you will bear it alone. *Proverbs 9:10–12* NKJV

**PRAYER:** O LORD, our God, other lords besides you have ruled over us, but your name alone do we honor. *Isaiah 26:13* NIV

**CHALLENGE:** Only conduct yourselves in a manner worthy of the gospel of Christ so that—whether I come and see you or whether I remain absent—I should hear that you are standing firm in one spirit, with one mind, by contending side by side for the faith of the gospel, [28]and by not being intimidated in any way by your opponents. This is a sign of their destruction, but of your salvation—a sign which is from God. *Philippians 1:27–28* NET

## ᔥ MAY 7 ᔥ

*Memory Verse 9*

**PROMISE:** So place yourselves under God's authority. Resist the devil, and he will run away from you. *James 4:7* GWORD

**PRAYER:** Answer me when I call to you, O my righteous God. Give me relief from my distress; be merciful to me and hear my prayer. *Psalms 4:1* NIV

**CHALLENGE:** Do not turn to idols or make for yourselves any gods of cast metal: I am the LORD your God. *Leviticus 19:4* ESV

## ᔥ MAY 8 ᔥ

*Memory Verse 9*

**PROMISE:** And my God will supply your every need according to his glorious riches in Christ Jesus. [20]May glory be given to God our Father forever and ever. Amen. *Philippians 4:19–20* NET

**PRAYER:** And the twenty-four elders who sit on their thrones before God fell on their faces and worshiped God, [17]saying, "We give thanks to you, Lord God Almighty, who is and who was, for you have taken your great power and begun to reign. [18]The nations raged, but your wrath came, and the time for the dead to be judged, and for rewarding your servants, the prophets and saints, and those who fear your name, both small and great, and for destroying the destroyers of the earth." *Revelation 11:16–18* ESV

**CHALLENGE:** Be merciful, just as your Father is merciful. *Luke 6:36* NET

## ஐ MAY 9 ல

*Memory Verse 10*

**PROMISE:** For whoever is ashamed of Me and of My words in this adulterous and sinful generation, the Son of Man will also be ashamed of him when He comes in the glory of His Father with the holy angels. *Mark 8:38* HCSB

**PRAYER:** Let the name of the LORD be praised, both now and for-evermore. ³From the rising of the sun to the place where it sets, the name of the LORD is to be praised. *Psalms 113:2–3* NIV

**CHALLENGE:** Dear friends, do not believe every spirit, but test the spirits to see whether they are from God, because many false proph-ets have gone out into the world. ²This is how you can recognize the Spirit of God: Every spirit that acknowledges that Jesus Christ has come in the flesh is from God, ³but every spirit that does not ac-knowledge Jesus is not from God. This is the spirit of the antichrist, which you have heard is coming and even now is already in the world. *1 John 4:1–3* NIV

## ஐ MAY 10 ல

*Memory Verse 10*

**PROMISE:** But when the Father sends the Advocate as my repre-sentative—that is, the Holy Spirit—he will teach you everything and will remind you of everything I have told you. ²⁷"I am leaving you with a gift—peace of mind and heart. And the peace I give is a gift the world cannot give. So don't be troubled or afraid. *John 14:26–27* NLT

**PRAYER:** "And when you pray, do not be like the hypocrites, for they love to pray standing in the synagogues and on the street corners to be seen by men. I tell you the truth, they have received their reward in full. *Matthew 6:5* NIV

**CHALLENGE:** Obey your leaders and submit to their authority. They keep watch over you as men who must give an account. Obey them so that their work will be a joy, not a burden, for that would be of no advantage to you. *Hebrews 13:17* NIV

## ℬ MAY 11 ℜ

### *Memory Verse 10*

**PROMISE:** And I heard a voice from heaven saying, "Write this down: Blessed are those who die in the Lord from now on. Yes, says the Spirit, they are blessed indeed, for they will rest from their hard work; for their good deeds follow them!" *Revelation 14:13* NLT

**PRAYER:** In my heart I store up your words, so I might not sin against you. *Psalms 119:11* NET

**CHALLENGE:** But Peter and John spoke right back, "Whether it's right in God's eyes to listen to you rather than to God, you decide. ²⁰As for us, there's no question—we can't keep quiet about what we've seen and heard." *Acts 4:19–20* MESSAGE

## ℬ MAY 12 ℜ

### *Memory Verse 10*

**PROMISE:** As God's partners, we beg you not to accept this marvelous gift of God's kindness and then ignore it. ²For God says, "At just the right time, I heard you. On the day of salvation, I helped you." Indeed, the "right time" is now. Today is the day of salvation. *2 Corinthians 6:1–2* NLT

**PRAYER:** By day the LORD directs his love, at night his song is with me—a prayer to the God of my life. *Psalms 42:8* NIV

**CHALLENGE:** Bless those who persecute you; bless and do not curse. ¹⁵Rejoice with those who rejoice; mourn with those who mourn. ¹⁶Live in harmony with one another. Do not be proud, but be willing to associate with people of low position. Do not be conceited. *Romans 12:14–16* NIV

## ✥ MAY 13 ✥

### *Memory Verse 10*

**PROMISE:** Then the sea gave up its dead, and Death and Hades gave up their dead; all were judged according to their works. ¹⁴Death and Hades were thrown into the lake of fire. This is the second death, the lake of fire. ¹⁵And anyone not found written in the book of life was thrown into the lake of fire. *Revelation 20:13–15* HCSB

**PRAYER:** Give me a desire for your rules, rather than for wealth gained unjustly. ³⁷Turn my eyes away from what is worthless! Revive me with your word! *Psalms 119:36–37* NET

**CHALLENGE:** "You shall have no other gods before me. *Exodus 20:3* NIV

## ✥ MAY 14 ✥

### *Memory Verse 10*

**PROMISE:** "Whoever, then, acknowledges me before people, I will acknowledge before my Father in heaven. ³³But whoever denies me before people, I will deny him also before my Father in heaven. *Matthew 10:32–33* NET

**PRAYER:** "My prayer is not for the world, but for those you have given me, because they belong to you. ¹⁰All who are mine belong to you, and you have given them to me, so they bring me glory. ¹¹Now I am departing from the world; they are staying in this world, but I am coming to you. Holy Father, you have given me your name; now protect them by the power of your name so that they will be united just as we are. *John 17:9–11* NLT

**CHALLENGE:** Preach the Word; be prepared in season and out of season; correct, rebuke and encourage—with great patience and careful instruction. *2 Timothy 4:2* NIV

## ഇ MAY 15 ൫

*Memory Verse 10*

**PROMISE:** For You rescue an afflicted people, but You humble those with haughty eyes. ²⁸LORD, You light my lamp; my God illuminates my darkness. *Psalms 18:27–28* HCSB

**PRAYER:** When they hurled their insults at him, he did not retaliate; when he suffered, he made no threats. Instead, he entrusted himself to him who judges justly. ²⁴He himself bore our sins in his body on the tree, so that we might die to sins and live for righteousness; by his wounds you have been healed. *1 Peter 2:23–24* NIV

**CHALLENGE:** For there is no distinction between the Jew and the Greek, for the same Lord is Lord of all, who richly blesses all who call on him. ¹³For everyone who calls on the name of the Lord will be saved. *Romans 10:12–13* NET

## ഇ MAY 16 ൫

*Memory Verse 10*

**PROMISE:** Look among the nations and watch. Be amazed and astonished. I am going to do something in your days that you would not believe even if it were reported to you. *Habakkuk 1:5* GWORD

**PRAYER:** Your right hand, O LORD, is glorious in power. Your right hand, O LORD, smashes the enemy. ⁷In the greatness of your majesty, you overthrow those who rise against you. You unleash your blazing fury; it consumes them like straw. *Exodus 15:6–7* NLT

**CHALLENGE:** Those who follow the right path fear the LORD; those who take the wrong path despise him. *Proverbs 14:2* NLT

## ಏ MAY **17** ಜ

*Memory Verse 10*

**PROMISE:** God is my strong fortress, and he makes my way perfect. *2 Samuel 22:33* NLT

**PRAYER:** But you are a shield around me, O LORD; you bestow glory on me and lift up my head. ⁴To the LORD I cry aloud, and he answers me from his holy hill. Selah *Psalms 3:3–4* NIV

**CHALLENGE:** Watch out for people who try to dazzle you with big words and intellectual double-talk. They want to drag you off into endless arguments that never amount to anything. They spread their ideas through the empty traditions of human beings and the empty superstitions of spirit beings. But that's not the way of Christ. *Colossians 2:8* MESSAGE

## ಏ MAY **18** ಜ

*Memory Verse 10*

**PROMISE:** Those who love money will never have enough. How meaningless to think that wealth brings true happiness! ¹¹The more you have, the more people come to help you spend it. So what good is wealth—except perhaps to watch it slip through your fingers! *Ecclesiastes 5:10–11* NLT

**PRAYER:** In my alarm I said, "I am cut off from your sight!" Yet you heard my cry for mercy when I called to you for help. *Psalms 31:22* NIV

**CHALLENGE:** Do not love the world or anything in the world. If anyone loves the world, the love of the Father is not in him. ¹⁶For everything in the world—the cravings of sinful man, the lust of his eyes and the boasting of what he has and does—comes not from the Father but from the world. *1 John 2:15–16* NIV

## ᔥ MAY 19 ᔥ

*Memory Verse 10*

**PROMISE:** "I tell you the truth, whatever you bind on earth will be bound in heaven, and whatever you loose on earth will be loosed in heaven. *Matthew 18:18* NIV

**PRAYER:** You have enlarged the nation, O LORD; you have enlarged the nation. You have gained glory for yourself; you have extended all the borders of the land. *Isaiah 26:15* NIV

**CHALLENGE:** The name of the Lord is a strong tower. A righteous person runs to it and is safe. *Proverbs 18:10* GWORD

## ᔥ MAY 20 ᔥ

*Memory Verse 10*

**PROMISE:** Now the Holy Spirit tells us clearly that in the last times some will turn away from the true faith; they will follow deceptive spirits and teachings that come from demons. ²These people are hypocrites and liars, and their consciences are dead. *1 Timothy 4:1–2* NLT

**PRAYER:** My steps have held fast to Your paths. My feet have not slipped. ⁶I have called upon You, for You will answer me, O God; Incline Your ear to me, hear my speech. *Psalms 17:5–6* NAS95

**CHALLENGE:** The result of humility is fear of the LORD, along with wealth, honor, and life. *Proverbs 22:4* HCSB

## ᔥ MAY 21 ᔥ

*Memory Verse 10*

**PROMISE:** Jesus answered, "Everyone who drinks this water will be thirsty again, ¹⁴but whoever drinks the water I give him will never thirst. Indeed, the water I give him will become in him a spring of water welling up to eternal life." *John 4:13–14* NIV

**PRAYER:** Give me understanding so that I might observe your law, and keep it with all my heart. ³⁵Guide me in the path of your commands, for I delight to walk in it. *Psalms 119:34–35* NET

**CHALLENGE:** Since you excel in so many ways—in your faith, your gifted speakers, your knowledge, your enthusiasm, and your love from us—I want you to excel also in this gracious act of giving. *2 Corinthians 8:7* NLT

## ℘ MAY 22 ℛ

### *Memory Verse 10*

**PROMISE:** If you will only obey me, you will have plenty to eat. ²⁰But if you turn away and refuse to listen, you will be devoured by the sword of your enemies. I, the LORD, have spoken!" *Isaiah 1:19–20* NLT

**PRAYER:** Great and marvelous are your works, O Lord God, the Almighty. Just and true are your ways, O King of the nations. ⁴Who will not fear you, Lord, and glorify your name? For you alone are holy. All nations will come and worship before you, for your righteous deeds have been revealed." *Revelation 15:3–4* NLT

**CHALLENGE:** Dear friend, do not imitate what is evil but what is good. Anyone who does what is good is from God. Anyone who does what is evil has not seen God. *3 John 1:11* NIV

## ℘ MAY 23 ℛ

### *Memory Verse 11*

**PROMISE:** He makes me as surefooted as a deer, enabling me to stand on mountain heights. ³⁵He trains my hands for battle; he strengthens my arm to draw a bronze bow. ³⁶You have given me your shield of victory; your help has made me great. *2 Samuel 22:34–36* NLT

**PRAYER:** I cry out to God Most High, to God, who fulfills [his purpose] for me. *Psalms 57:2* NIV

**CHALLENGE:** How are they to call on one they have not believed in? And how are they to believe in one they have not heard of? And how are they to hear without someone preaching to them? [15]And how are they to preach unless they are sent? As it is written, "How timely is the arrival of those who proclaim the good news." *Romans 10:14–15* NET

## ℰↃ MAY 24 ◯ℛ

### *Memory Verse 11*

**PROMISE:** The LORD is my portion; I have promised to keep Your words. *Psalms 119:57* NAS95

**PRAYER:** Now may our Lord Jesus Christ himself and God our Father, who loved us and by grace gave us eternal comfort and good hope, [17]encourage your hearts and strengthen you in every good thing you do or say. *2 Thessalonians 2:16–17* NET

**CHALLENGE:** Don't let evil conquer you, but conquer evil by doing good. *Romans 12:21* NLT

## ℰↃ MAY 25 ◯ℛ

### *Memory Verse 11*

**PROMISE:** The life of every living thing is in His hand, as well as the breath of all mankind. *Job 12:10* HCSB

**PRAYER:** Likewise the Spirit also helps in our weaknesses. For we do not know what we should pray for as we ought, but the Spirit Himself makes intercession for us with groanings which cannot be uttered. *Romans 8:26* NKJV

**CHALLENGE:** Give to the Lord, you families of the nations. Give to the Lord glory and power. [8]Give to the Lord the glory he deserves. Bring an offering, and come into his courtyards. *Psalms 96:7–8* GWORD

# ∽ MAY 26 ∾

## *Memory Verse 11*

**PROMISE:** And while they were gathering together in Galilee, Jesus said to them, "The Son of Man is going to be delivered into the hands of men; ²³and they will kill Him, and He will be raised on the third day." And they were deeply grieved. *Matthew 17:22–23* NAS95

**PRAYER:** Arise, O LORD! Deliver me, O my God! Strike all my enemies on the jaw; break the teeth of the wicked. *Psalms 3:7* NIV

**CHALLENGE:** Therefore be alert, since you don't know when the master of the house is coming—whether in the evening or at midnight or at the crowing of the rooster or early in the morning. ³⁶Otherwise, he might come suddenly and find you sleeping. ³⁷And what I say to you, I say to everyone: Be alert!" *Mark 13:35–37* HCSB

# ∽ MAY 27 ∾

## *Memory Verse 11*

**PROMISE:** There is no favoritism with God. ¹²All those who sinned without the law will also perish without the law, and all those who sinned under the law will be judged by the law. ¹³For the hearers of the law are not righteous before God, but the doers of the law will be declared righteous. *Romans 2:11–13* HCSB

**PRAYER:** I have experienced times of need and times of abundance. In any and every circumstance I have learned the secret of contentment, whether I go satisfied or hungry, have plenty or nothing. ¹³I am able to do all things through the one who strengthens me. *Philippians 4:12–13* NET

**CHALLENGE:** If I then, your Lord and Teacher, have washed your feet, you also ought to wash one another's feet. ¹⁵For I have given you an example, that you should do as I have done to you. *John 13:14–15* NKJV

## ॐ MAY 28 ॐ

*Memory Verse 11*

**PROMISE:** The LORD will not allow the righteous to hunger, But He will reject the craving of the wicked. *Proverbs 10:3* NAS95

**PRAYER:** "I have revealed you to the ones you gave me from this world. They were always yours. You gave them to me, and they have kept your word. ⁷Now they know that everything I have is a gift from you, ⁸for I have passed on to them the message you gave me. They accepted it and know that I came from you, and they believe you sent me. *John 17:6–8* NLT

**CHALLENGE:** Commit your future to the LORD! Trust in him, and he will act on your behalf. *Psalms 37:5* NET

## ॐ MAY 29 ॐ

*Memory Verse 11*

**PROMISE:** "You are my witnesses," declares the LORD, "and my servant whom I have chosen, that you may know and believe me and understand that I am he. Before me no god was formed, nor shall there be any after me. ¹¹I, I am the LORD, and besides me there is no savior. *Isaiah 43:10–11* ESV

**PRAYER:** For by grace you have been saved through faith; and that not of yourselves, it is the gift of God; ⁹not as a result of works, so that no one may boast. *Ephesians 2:8–9* NAS95

**CHALLENGE:** Entrust your efforts to the Lord, and your plans will succeed. *Proverbs 16:3* GWORD

## ᔓ MAY **30** ᔕ

*Memory Verse 11*

**PROMISE:** If you live by your corrupt nature, you are going to die. But if you use your spiritual nature to put to death the evil activities of the body, you will live. *Romans 8:13* GWORD

**PRAYER:** Blessing and honor and glory and dominion to the One seated on the throne, and to the Lamb, forever and ever! *Revelation 5:13* HCSB

**CHALLENGE:** Let your eyes look straight ahead, fix your gaze directly before you. [26]Make level paths for your feet and take only ways that are firm. *Proverbs 4:25–26* NIV

## ᔓ MAY **31** ᔕ

*Memory Verse 11*

**PROMISE:** The LORD reigns, He is clothed with majesty; The LORD is clothed, He has girded Himself with strength. Surely the world is established, so that it cannot be moved. *Psalms 93:1* NKJV

**PRAYER:** Then I heard someone from the altar say: Yes, Lord God, the Almighty, true and righteous are Your judgments. *Revelation 16:7* HCSB

**CHALLENGE:** Stay away from fools, for you won't find knowledge on their lips. *Proverbs 14:7* NLT

# June

## ᔥ JUNE 1 ᔐ

*Memory Verse 11*

**PROMISE:** The rich and the poor have this in common: the LORD made them both. *Proverbs 22:2* HCSB

**PRAYER:** Let the heavens be glad, and let the earth rejoice, and let them say among the nations, "The LORD reigns!" *1 Chronicles 16:31* ESV

**CHALLENGE:** So you, my child, be strong in the grace that is in Christ Jesus. ²And entrust what you heard me say in the presence of many others as witnesses to faithful people who will be competent to teach others as well. ³Take your share of suffering as a good soldier of Christ Jesus. ⁴No one in military service gets entangled in matters of everyday life; otherwise he will not please the one who recruited him. *2 Timothy 2:1–4* NET

## ᔥ JUNE 2 ᔐ

*Memory Verse 11*

**PROMISE:** He who finds a wife finds a good thing and obtains favor from the LORD. *Proverbs 18:22* ESV

**PRAYER:** Turn your ear to me, come quickly to my rescue; be my rock of refuge, a strong fortress to save me. *Psalms 31:2* NIV

**CHALLENGE:** Go easy on those who hesitate in the faith. ²³Go after those who take the wrong way. Be tender with sinners, but not soft on sin. The sin itself stinks to high heaven. *Jude 1:22–23* MESSAGE

## ဢ JUNE 3 ရ

*Memory Verse 11*

**PROMISE:** Remember what I told you: I am going away, but I will come back to you again. If you really loved me, you would be happy that I am going to the Father, who is greater than I am. *John 14:28* NLT

**PRAYER:** Out of the depths I cry to you, O LORD; ²O Lord, hear my voice. Let your ears be attentive to my cry for mercy. *Psalms 130:1–2* NIV

**CHALLENGE:** And we urge you, brothers and sisters, admonish the undisciplined, comfort the discouraged, help the weak, be patient toward all. *1 Thessalonians 5:14* NET

## ဢ JUNE 4 ရ

*Memory Verse 11*

**PROMISE:** ⁴⁰As the weeds are collected and burned with fire, so it will be at the end of the age. ⁴¹The Son of Man will send his angels, and they will gather from his kingdom everything that causes sin as well as all lawbreakers. ⁴²They will throw them into the fiery furnace, where there will be weeping and gnashing of teeth. ⁴³Then the righteous will shine like the sun in the kingdom of their Father. The one who has ears had better listen! *Matthew 13:39–43* NET

**PRAYER:** "You have also given me the shield of Your salvation; Your gentleness has made me great. ³⁷You enlarged my path under me; So my feet did not slip. *2 Samuel 22:36–37* NKJV

**CHALLENGE:** Never steal, lie, or deceive your neighbor. ¹²"Never swear by my name in order to deceive anyone. This dishonors the name of your God. I am the Lord. *Leviticus 19:11–12* GWORD

# ℘ JUNE 5 ℃

*Memory Verse 11*

**PROMISE:** Talk is cheap, like daydreams and other useless activities. Fear God instead. *Ecclesiastes 5:7* NLT

**PRAYER:** Deliver me from oppressive men, so that I can keep your precepts. ¹³⁵Smile on your servant! Teach me your statutes! ¹³⁶Tears stream down from my eyes, because people do not keep your law. *Psalms 119:134–136* NET

**CHALLENGE:** And He answered and said, "Have you not read that He who created them from the beginning MADE THEM MALE AND FEMALE, ⁵and said, 'FOR THIS REASON A MAN SHALL LEAVE HIS FATHER AND MOTHER AND BE JOINED TO HIS WIFE, AND THE TWO SHALL BECOME ONE FLESH'? ⁶"So they are no longer two, but one flesh. What therefore God has joined together, let no man separate." *Matthew 19:4–6* NAS95

# ℘ JUNE 6 ℃

*Memory Verse 12*

**PROMISE:** Then I heard a loud voice from the throne: Look! God's dwelling is with humanity, and He will live with them. They will be His people, and God Himself will be with them and be their God. *Revelation 21:3* HCSB

**PRAYER:** Judge me, O God, and plead my cause against an ungodly nation: O deliver me from the deceitful and unjust man. *Psalms 43:1* KJV

**CHALLENGE:** See that no one pays back evil for evil to anyone, but always pursue what is good for one another and for all. *1 Thessalonians 5:15* NET

## ᏽ JUNE 7 ᏸ

*Memory Verse 12*

**PROMISE:** The world and its desires pass away, but the man who does the will of God lives forever. *1 John 2:17* NIV

**PRAYER:** Who is like you among the gods, O LORD glorious in holiness, awesome in splendor, performing great wonders? ¹²You raised your right hand, and the earth swallowed our enemies. *Exodus 15:11–12* NLT

**CHALLENGE:** Finally, my brethren, be strong in the Lord, and in the power of his might. *Ephesians 6:10* KJV

## ᏽ JUNE 8 ᏸ

*Memory Verse 12*

**PROMISE:** Do not waste time arguing over godless ideas and old wives' tales. Instead, train yourself to be godly. ⁸"Physical training is good, but training for godliness is much better, promising benefits in this life and in the life to come." *1 Timothy 4:7–8* NLT

**PRAYER:** But you, O God, will bring down the wicked into the pit of corruption; bloodthirsty and deceitful men will not live out half their days. But as for me, I trust in you. *Psalms 55:23* NIV

**CHALLENGE:** So rid yourselves of all malice, all deceit, hypocrisy, envy, and all slander. *1 Peter 2:1* HCSB

## ᏽ JUNE 9 ᏸ

*Memory Verse 12*

**PROMISE:** The Lord made you, formed you in the womb, and will help you. This is what the Lord says: Don't be afraid, my servant Jacob, Jeshurun, whom I have chosen. ³I will pour water on thirsty ground and rain on dry land. I will pour my Spirit on your offspring and my blessing on your descendants. *Isaiah 44:2–3* GWORD

**PRAYER:** The LORD is my portion, saith my soul; therefore will I hope in him. *Lamentations 3:24* KJV

**CHALLENGE:** Well then, if you teach others, why don't you teach yourself? You tell others not to steal, but do you steal? [22]You say it is wrong to commit adultery, but do you commit adultery? You condemn idolatry, but do you use items stolen from pagan temples? *Romans 2:21–22* NLT

## ᕙ JUNE 10 ᕗ

*Memory Verse 12*

**PROMISE:** No wisdom, no understanding, and no counsel will prevail against the LORD. *Proverbs 21:30* HCSB

**PRAYER:** Consider therefore the kindness and sternness of God: sternness to those who fell, but kindness to you, provided that you continue in his kindness. Otherwise, you also will be cut off. *Romans 11:22* NIV

**CHALLENGE:** Love the Lord your God with all your heart, with all your soul, and with all your strength. [6]Take to heart these words that I give you today. *Deuteronomy 6:5–6* GWORD

## ᕙ JUNE 11 ᕗ

*Memory Verse 12*

**PROMISE:** You have given me the shield of your salvation. Your right hand supports me. Your gentleness makes me great. *Psalms 18:35* GWORD

**PRAYER:** "Again, I tell you that if two of you on earth agree about anything you ask for, it will be done for you by my Father in heaven. [20]For where two or three come together in my name, there am I with them." *Matthew 18:19–20* NIV

**CHALLENGE:** You must each decide in your heart how much to give. And don't give reluctantly or in response to pressure. "For God loves a person who gives cheerfully." *2 Corinthians 9:7* NLT

## ❧ JUNE 12 ❧

### *Memory Verse 12*

**PROMISE:** For simpletons turn away from me—to death. Fools are destroyed by their own complacency. ³³But all who listen to me will live in peace, untroubled by fear of harm." ¹My child, listen to what I say, and treasure my commands. *Proverbs 1:32–2:1* NLT

**PRAYER:** Heal me, O Lord, and I will be healed. Rescue me, and I will be rescued. You are the one I praise. *Jeremiah 17:14* GWORD

**CHALLENGE:** Now it is required that those who have been given a trust must prove faithful. ³I care very little if I am judged by you or by any human court; indeed, I do not even judge myself. ⁴My conscience is clear, but that does not make me innocent. It is the Lord who judges me. ⁵Therefore judge nothing before the appointed time; wait till the Lord comes. He will bring to light what is hidden in darkness and will expose the motives of men's hearts. At that time each will receive his praise from God. *1 Corinthians 4:2–5* NIV

## ❧ JUNE 13 ❧

### *Memory Verse 12*

**PROMISE:** Jesus was curt: "You yourself said it. And that's not all. Soon you'll see it for yourself: The Son of Man seated at the right hand of the Mighty One, Arriving on the clouds of heaven." *Matthew 26:64* MESSAGE

**PRAYER:** I brought glory to you here on earth by completing the work you gave me to do. ⁵Now, Father, bring me into the glory we shared before the world began. *John 17:4–5* NLT

**CHALLENGE:** Worship the Lord in ‹his› holy splendor. Tremble in his presence, all the earth! ¹⁰Say to the nations, "The Lord rules as king!" The earth stands firm; it cannot be moved. He will judge people fairly. *Psalms 96:9–10* GWORD

## ஐ JUNE 14 ௸

*Memory Verse 12*

**PROMISE:** "The LORD lives! Blessed be my Rock! Let God be exalted, The Rock of my salvation! *2 Samuel 22:47* NKJV

**PRAYER:** Nevertheless I am continually with You; You have taken hold of my right hand. ²⁴With Your counsel You will guide me, And afterward receive me to glory. *Psalms 73:23–24* NAS95

**CHALLENGE:** It is a sin to belittle one's neighbor; blessed are those who help the poor. *Proverbs 14:21* NLT

## ஐ JUNE 15 ௸

*Memory Verse 12*

**PROMISE:** Wisdom and strength belong to God; counsel and understanding are His. ¹⁴Whatever He tears down cannot be rebuilt; whoever He imprisons cannot be released. ¹⁵When He withholds the waters, everything dries up, and when He releases them, they destroy the land. *Job 12:13–15* HCSB

**PRAYER:** O send out Your light and Your truth, let them lead me; Let them bring me to Your holy hill And to Your dwelling places. ⁴Then I will go to the altar of God, To God my exceeding joy; And upon the lyre I shall praise You, O God, my God. *Psalms 43:3–4* NAS95

**CHALLENGE:** "Look at the proud! They trust in themselves, and their lives are crooked. But the righteous will live by their faithfulness to God. *Habakkuk 2:4* NLT

## ഌ JUNE 16 ☯

*Memory Verse 12*

**PROMISE:** He has removed our sins as far from us as the east is from the west. *Psalms 103:12* NLT

**PRAYER:** We're all like sheep who've wandered off and gotten lost. We've all done our own thing, gone our own way. And GOD has piled all our sins, everything we've done wrong, on him, on him. *Isaiah 53:6* MESSAGE

**CHALLENGE:** This is the message you heard from the beginning: We should love one another. *1 John 3:11* NIV

## ഌ JUNE 17 ☯

*Memory Verse 12*

**PROMISE:** For one who has died has been set free from sin. ⁸Now if we have died with Christ, we believe that we will also live with him. ⁹We know that Christ, being raised from the dead, will never die again; death no longer has dominion over him. ¹⁰For the death he died he died to sin, once for all, but the life he lives he lives to God. ¹¹So you also must consider yourselves dead to sin and alive to God in Christ Jesus. *Romans 6:7–11* ESV

**PRAYER:** If you, O LORD, kept a record of sins, O Lord, who could stand? ⁴But with you there is forgiveness; therefore you are feared. *Psalms 130:3–4* NIV

**CHALLENGE:** My sheep listen to my voice; I know them, and they follow me *John 10:27* NLT

## ৯০ JUNE 18 ৫৪

*Memory Verse 12*

**PROMISE:** This letter is from Paul, a slave of God and an apostle of Jesus Christ. I have been sent to proclaim faith to those God has chosen and to teach them to know the truth that shows them how to live godly lives. ²This truth gives them confidence that they have eternal life, which God—who does not lie—promised them before the world began. ³And now at just the right time he has revealed this message, which we announce to everyone. It is by the command of God our Savior that I have been entrusted with this work for him. *Titus 1:1–3* NLT

**PRAYER:** For You, LORD, have made me glad through Your work; I will triumph in the works of Your hands. ⁵O LORD, how great are Your works! Your thoughts are very deep. *Psalms 92:4–5* NKJV

**CHALLENGE:** The plans of the heart belong to humans, but an answer on the tongue comes from the Lord. ²A person thinks all his ways are pure, but the Lord weighs motives. *Proverbs 16:1–2* GWORD

## ৯০ JUNE 19 ৫৪

*Memory Verse 12*

**PROMISE:** But Jesus said, "Let the children alone, and do not hinder them from coming to Me; for the kingdom of heaven belongs to such as these." ¹⁵After laying His hands on them, He departed from there. *Matthew 19:14–15* NAS95

**PRAYER:** I run along the path of your commands, for you enable me to do so. ³³(He) Teach me, O LORD, the lifestyle prescribed by your statutes, so that I might observe it continually. *Psalms 119:32–33* NET

**CHALLENGE:** "Let not your heart be troubled; you believe in God, believe also in Me. *John 14:1* NKJV

## ஐ JUNE 20 ର

*Memory Verse 13*

**PROMISE:** For the Lord Himself will descend from heaven with a shout, with the archangel's voice, and with the trumpet of God, and the dead in Christ will rise first. ¹⁷Then we who are still alive will be caught up together with them in the clouds to meet the Lord in the air and so we will always be with the Lord. *1 Thessalonians 4:16–17* HCSB

**PRAYER:** O LORD, you have examined my heart and know everything about me. ²You know when I sit down or stand up. You know my thoughts even when I'm far away. *Psalms 139:1–2* NLT

**CHALLENGE:** He who guards his mouth and his tongue, Guards his soul from troubles. *Proverbs 21:23* NAS95

## ஐ JUNE 21 ର

*Memory Verse 13*

**PROMISE:** The LORD's curse is on the house of the wicked, but he blesses the home of the righteous. ³⁴He mocks proud mockers but gives grace to the humble. *Proverbs 3:33–34* NIV

**PRAYER:** When you ask for something, don't have any doubts. A person who has doubts is like a wave that is blown by the wind and tossed by the sea. ⁷A person who has doubts shouldn't expect to receive anything from the Lord. ⁸A person who has doubts is thinking about two different things at the same time and can't make up his mind about anything. *James 1:6–8* GWORD

**CHALLENGE:** Will the LORD be pleased with thousands of rams, with ten thousands of rivers of oil? Shall I give my firstborn for my transgression, the fruit of my body for the sin of my soul?" ⁸He has told you, O man, what is good; and what does the LORD require of you but to do justice, and to love kindness, and to walk humbly with your God? *Micah 6:7–8* ESV

## ☙ JUNE 22 ❧

*Memory Verse 13*

**PROMISE:** "Do not judge, or you too will be judged. ²For in the same way you judge others, you will be judged, and with the measure you use, it will be measured to you. *Matthew 7:1–2* NIV

**PRAYER:** But I call to God, and the LORD saves me. ¹⁷Evening, morning and noon I cry out in distress, and he hears my voice. *Psalms 55:16–17* NIV

**CHALLENGE:** Jesus *said to her, "Your brother will rise again." ²⁴Martha *said to Him, "I know that he will rise again in the resurrection on the last day." ²⁵Jesus said to her, "I am the resurrection and the life; he who believes in Me will live even if he dies, ²⁶and everyone who lives and believes in Me will never die. Do you believe this?" *John 11:23–26* NAS95

## ☙ JUNE 23 ❧

*Memory Verse 13*

**PROMISE:** Work brings profit, but mere talk leads to poverty! ²⁴Wealth is a crown for the wise; the effort of fools yields only foolishness. *Proverbs 14:23–24* NLT

**PRAYER:** Oh, the depth of the riches of the wisdom and knowledge of God! How unsearchable his judgments, and his paths beyond tracing out! *Romans 11:33–34* NIV

**CHALLENGE:** "If I glorify Myself," Jesus answered, "My glory is nothing. My Father—you say about Him, 'He is our God'—He is the One who glorifies Me. ⁵⁵You've never known Him, but I know Him. If I were to say I don't know Him, I would be a liar like you. But I do know Him, and I keep His word. *John 8:54–55* HCSB

## ೫ JUNE **24** ೫

*Memory Verse 13*

**PROMISE:** Every way of a man is right in his own eyes, But the LORD weighs the hearts. *Proverbs 21:2* NKJV

**PRAYER:** With your unfailing love you lead the people you have redeemed. In your might, you guide them to your sacred home. *Exodus 15:13* NLT

**CHALLENGE:** Then Jesus came to them and said, "All authority in heaven and on earth has been given to me. ¹⁹Therefore go and make disciples of all nations, baptizing them in the name of the Father and of the Son and of the Holy Spirit, ²⁰and teaching them to obey everything I have commanded you. And surely I am with you always, to the very end of the age." *Matthew 28:18–20* NIV

## ೫ JUNE **25** ೫

*Memory Verse 13*

**PROMISE:** And we know that God causes everything to work together for the good of those who love God and are called according to his purpose for them. *Romans 8:28* NLT

**PRAYER:** For I will not trust in my bow, Nor shall my sword save me. ⁷But You have saved us from our enemies, And have put to shame those who hated us. ⁸In God we boast all day long, And praise Your name forever. Selah *Psalms 44:6–8* NKJV

**CHALLENGE:** The lips of the wise spread knowledge, But the hearts of fools are not so. *Proverbs 15:7* NAS95

## ഇ JUNE 26 ൏

*Memory Verse 13*

**PROMISE:** "Look, I will come as unexpectedly as a thief! Blessed are all who are watching for me, who keep their clothing ready so they will not have to walk around naked and ashamed." *Revelation 16:15* NLT

**PRAYER:** Your justice endures, and your law is reliable. ¹⁴³Distress and hardship confront me, yet I find delight in your commands. *Psalms 119:142–143* NET

**CHALLENGE:** And let the peace of the Messiah, to which you were also called in one body, control your hearts. Be thankful. ¹⁶Let the message about the Messiah dwell richly among you, teaching and admonishing one another in all wisdom, and singing psalms, hymns, and spiritual songs, with gratitude in your hearts to God. ¹⁷And whatever you do, in word or in deed, do everything in the name of the Lord Jesus, giving thanks to God the Father through Him. *Colossians 3:15–17* HCSB

## ഇ JUNE 27 ൏

*Memory Verse 13*

**PROMISE:** Lazy hands bring poverty, but hard-working hands bring riches. ⁵Whoever gathers in the summer is a wise son. Whoever sleeps at harvest time brings shame. *Proverbs 10:4–5* GWORD

**PRAYER:** Blessed be the LORD God, the God of Israel, Who alone works wonders. ¹⁹And blessed be His glorious name forever; And may the whole earth be filled with His glory. Amen, and Amen. *Psalms 72:18–19* NAS95

**CHALLENGE:** My confident hope is that I will in no way be ashamed but that with complete boldness, even now as always, Christ will be exalted in my body, whether I live or die. ²¹For to me, living is Christ and dying is gain. *Philippians 1:20–21* NET

## ℘ JUNE 28 ℧

*Memory Verse 13*

**PROMISE:** ¹⁴For all who are led by the Spirit of God are sons of God. ¹⁵For you did not receive the spirit of slavery to fall back into fear, but you have received the Spirit of adoption as sons, by whom we cry, "Abba! Father!" *Romans 8:13–15* ESV

**PRAYER:** Indeed it was for my own peace That I had great bitterness; But You have lovingly delivered my soul from the pit of corruption, For You have cast all my sins behind Your back. *Isaiah 38:17* NKJV

**CHALLENGE:** Avoid godless chatter, because those who indulge in it will become more and more ungodly. *2 Timothy 2:16* NIV

## ℘ JUNE 29 ℧

*Memory Verse 13*

**PROMISE:** He who testifies to these things says, "Surely I am coming quickly." Amen. Even so, come, Lord Jesus! *Revelation 22:20* NKJV

**PRAYER:** Be merciful to me, O God, for men hotly pursue me; all day long they press their attack. ²My slanderers pursue me all day long; many are attacking me in their pride. *Psalms 56:1–2* NIV

**CHALLENGE:** Go to the Temple and give the people this message of life!" *Acts 5:20* NLT

## ℘ JUNE 30 ℧

*Memory Verse 13*

**PROMISE:** "Ask and it will be given to you; seek and you will find; knock and the door will be opened for you. ⁸For everyone who asks receives, and the one who seeks finds, and to the one who knocks, the door will be opened. *Matthew 7:7–8* NET

**PRAYER:** The LORD will work out his plans for my life—for your faithful love, O LORD, endures forever. Don't abandon me, for you made me. *Psalms 138:8* NLT

**CHALLENGE:** Rather, love your enemies, help them, and lend to them without expecting to get anything back. Then you will have a great reward. You will be the children of the Most High God. After all, he is kind to unthankful and evil people. *Luke 6:35* GWORD

# July

## ℘ JULY 1 ℘

*Memory Verse 13*

**PROMISE:** A peaceful heart leads to a healthy body; jealousy is like cancer in the bones. *Proverbs 14:30* NLT

**PRAYER:** But when you pray, go into your room, close the door and pray to your Father, who is unseen. Then your Father, who sees what is done in secret, will reward you. *Matthew 6:6* NIV

**CHALLENGE:** Dear friends, let us love one another, for love comes from God. Everyone who loves has been born of God and knows God. ⁸Whoever does not love does not know God, because God is love. *1 John 4:7–8* NIV

## ℘ JULY 2 ℘

*Memory Verse 13*

**PROMISE:** This saying is trustworthy and deserving of full acceptance: "Christ Jesus came into the world to save sinners"—and I am the worst of them. ¹⁶But I received mercy for this reason, so that in me, the worst of them, Christ Jesus might demonstrate His extraordinary patience as an example to those who would believe in Him for eternal life. *1 Timothy 1:15–17* HCSB

**PRAYER:** "Praise our God, all his servants, all who fear him, from the least to the greatest." *Revelation 19:5* NLT

**CHALLENGE:** Seeing then that we have a great High Priest who has passed through the heavens, Jesus the Son of God, let us hold fast our confession. ¹⁵For we do not have a High Priest who cannot sympathize with our weaknesses, but was in all points tempted as we are, yet without sin. ¹⁶Let us therefore come boldly to the throne of grace, that we may obtain mercy and find grace to help in time of need. *Hebrews 4:14–16* NKJV

## ஐ JULY 3 ର

### *Memory Verse 13*

**PROMISE:** Sustain me as you promised, so that I will live. Do not disappoint me! ¹¹⁷Support me, so that I will be delivered. Then I will focus on your statutes continually. *Psalms 119:116–117* NET

**PRAYER:** I thank my God every time I remember you. ⁴I always pray with joy in my every prayer for all of you ⁵because of your participation in the gospel from the first day until now. *Philippians 1:3–5* NET

**CHALLENGE:** Never gossip. Never endanger your neighbor's life. I am the Lord. *Leviticus 19:16* GWORD

## ஐ JULY 4 ର

### *Memory Verse 14*

**PROMISE:** But when they looked up, they saw that the stone had been rolled away—for it was very large. ⁵And entering the tomb, they saw a young man clothed in a long white robe sitting on the right side; and they were alarmed. ⁶But he said to them, "Do not be alarmed. You seek Jesus of Nazareth, who was crucified. He is risen! He is not here. See the place where they laid Him. ⁷But go, tell His disciples—and Peter—that He is going before you into Galilee; there you will see Him, as He said to you." *Mark 16:4–7* NKJV

**PRAYER:** Then Nebuchadnezzar said, "Praise to the God of Shadrach, Meshach, and Abednego! He sent his angel to rescue his servants who trusted in him. They defied the king's command and were willing to die rather than serve or worship any god except their own God. *Daniel 3:28* NLT

**CHALLENGE:** Don't say, "I will avenge this evil!" Wait on the LORD, and He will rescue you. *Proverbs 20:22* HCSB

## ℘ JULY 5 ℭ

### *Memory Verse 14*

**PROMISE:** You were dead because of your sins and because your sinful nature was not yet cut away. Then God made you alive with Christ, for he forgave all our sins. ¹⁴He canceled the record of the charges against us and took it away by nailing it to the cross. ¹⁵In this way, he disarmed the spiritual rulers and authorities. He shamed them publicly by his victory over them on the cross. *Colossians 2:13–15* NLT

**PRAYER:** For You have armed me with strength for the battle; You have subdued under me those who rose up against me. *Psalms 18:39* NKJV

**CHALLENGE:** When you make a promise to God, don't delay in following through, for God takes no pleasure in fools. Keep all the promises you make to him. ⁵It is better to say nothing than to make a promise and not keep it. *Ecclesiastes 5:4–5* NLT

## ℘ JULY 6 ℭ

### *Memory Verse 14*

**PROMISE:** And this is the way to have eternal life—to know you, the only true God, and Jesus Christ, the one you sent to earth. *John 17:3* NLT

**PRAYER:** Have mercy on me, O God, have mercy on me, for in you my soul takes refuge. I will take refuge in the shadow of your wings until the disaster has passed. *Psalms 57:1* NIV

**CHALLENGE:** "You shall not make for yourself an idol in the form of anything in heaven above or on the earth beneath or in the waters below. ⁵You shall not bow down to them or worship them; for I, the LORD your God, am a jealous God, punishing the children for the sin of the fathers to the third and fourth generation of those who hate me, ⁶but showing love to a thousand [generations] of those who love me and keep my commandments. *Exodus 20:4–6* NIV

## ഇ JULY 7 ൏

*Memory Verse 14*

**PROMISE:** "Now I will arise," says the LORD, "Now I will be exalted, now I will be lifted up. *Isaiah 33:10* NAS95

**PRAYER:** He delivers me from my enemies. You also lift me up above those who rise against me; You have delivered me from the violent man. ⁵⁰Therefore I will give thanks to You, O LORD, among the Gentiles, And sing praises to Your name. *2 Samuel 22:49–50* NKJV

**CHALLENGE:** Figure out what will please Christ, and then do it. ¹¹Don't waste your time on useless work, mere busywork, the barren pursuits of darkness. Expose these things for the sham they are. ¹²It's a scandal when people waste their lives on things they must do in the darkness where no one will see. ¹³Rip the cover off those frauds and see how attractive they look in the light of Christ. *Ephesians 5:10–13* MESSAGE

## ഇ JULY 8 ൏

*Memory Verse 14*

**PROMISE:** The LORD shall reign for ever and ever. *Exodus 15:18* KJV

**PRAYER:** I choose the path of faithfulness; I am committed to your regulations. ³¹I hold fast to your rules. O LORD, do not let me be ashamed! *Psalms 119:30–31* NET

**CHALLENGE:** For every kind of beast and bird, of reptile and sea creature, can be tamed and has been tamed by mankind, *8*but no human being can tame the tongue. It is a restless evil, full of deadly poison. *9*With it we bless our Lord and Father, and with it we curse people who are made in the likeness of God. *10*From the same mouth come blessing and cursing. My brothers, these things ought not to be so. *James 3:7–10* ESV

## ஒ JULY 9 ௸

*Memory Verse 14*

**PROMISE:** Whoever knows what is right but doesn't do it is sinning. *James 4:17* GWORD

**PRAYER:** Therefore You are great, O Lord GOD. For there is none like You, nor is there any God besides You, according to all that we have heard with our ears. *2 Samuel 7:22* NKJV

**CHALLENGE:** So flee youthful passions and pursue righteousness, faith, love, and peace, along with those who call on the Lord from a pure heart. *23*Have nothing to do with foolish, ignorant controversies; you know that they breed quarrels. *24*And the Lord's servant must not be quarrelsome but kind to everyone, able to teach, patiently enduring evil, *2 Timothy 2:22–24* ESV

## ஒ JULY 10 ௸

*Memory Verse 14*

**PROMISE:** Everything is clean to those who are clean. But nothing is clean to corrupt unbelievers. Indeed, their minds and their consciences are corrupted. *16*They claim to know God, but they deny him by what they do. They are detestable, disobedient, and unfit to do anything good. *Titus 1:15–16* GWORD

**PRAYER:** Let the sea roar, and all that fills it; let the field exult, and everything in it! *33*Then shall the trees of the forest sing for joy before the LORD, for he comes to judge the earth. ³⁴Oh give thanks to the LORD, for he is good; for his steadfast love endures forever! *1 Chronicles 16:32–34* ESV

**CHALLENGE:** Put away perversity from your mouth; keep corrupt talk far from your lips. *Proverbs 4:24* NIV

## ✆ JULY 11 ✆

*Memory Verse 14*

**PROMISE:** "Man who is born of woman Is of few days and full of trouble. ²He comes forth like a flower and fades away; He flees like a shadow and does not continue. *Job 14:1–2* NKJV

**PRAYER:** Then he returned to the disciples and found them asleep. He said to Peter, "Couldn't you watch with me even one hour? ⁴¹Keep watch and pray, so that you will not give in to temptation. For the spirit is willing, but the body is weak!" *Matthew 26:40–41* NLT

**CHALLENGE:** The one who reveals secrets is a constant gossip; avoid someone with a big mouth. *Proverbs 20:19* HCSB

## ✆ JULY 12 ✆

*Memory Verse 14*

**PROMISE:** You are near, O LORD, and all your commands are reliable. ¹⁵²I learned long ago that you ordained your rules to last. *Psalms 119:151–152* NET

**PRAYER:** Forget what happened in the past, and do not dwell on events from long ago. ¹⁹I am going to do something new. It is already happening. Don't you recognize it? I will clear a way in the desert. I will make rivers on dry land. *Isaiah 43:18–19* GWORD

**CHALLENGE:** When Jesus saw what was happening, he was angry with his disciples. He said to them, "Let the children come to me. Don't stop them! For the Kingdom of God belongs to those who are like these children. <sup>15</sup>I tell you the truth, anyone who doesn't receive the Kingdom of God like a child will never enter it." *Mark 10:14–15* NLT

## ᔭᔪ JULY 13 ᔭᔪ

### *Memory Verse 14*

**PROMISE:** Behold, the days are coming, declares the LORD, when I will fulfill the promise I made to the house of Israel and the house of Judah. *Jeremiah 33:14* ESV

**PRAYER:** Oh, what joy for those whose disobedience is forgiven, whose sins are put out of sight. <sup>8</sup>Yes, what joy for those whose record the LORD has cleared of sin." *Romans 4:7–8* NLT

**CHALLENGE:** For no one can lay any other foundation than what has been laid down. That foundation is Jesus Christ. <sup>12</sup>If anyone builds on that foundation with gold, silver, costly stones, wood, hay, or straw, <sup>13</sup>each one's work will become obvious, for the day will disclose it, because it will be revealed by fire; the fire will test the quality of each one's work. *1 Corinthians 3:11–13* HCSB

## ᔭᔪ JULY 14 ᔭᔪ

### *Memory Verse 14*

**PROMISE:** He will wipe away every tear from their eyes. Death will no longer exist; grief, crying, and pain will exist no longer, because the previous things have passed away. *Revelation 21:4* HCSB

**PRAYER:** or WHO HAS KNOWN THE MIND OF THE LORD, OR WHO BECAME HIS COUNSELOR? <sup>35</sup>Or WHO HAS FIRST GIVEN TO HIM THAT IT MIGHT BE PAID BACK TO HIM AGAIN? <sup>36</sup>For from Him and through Him and to Him are all things. To Him be the glory forever. Amen. *Romans 11:34–36* NAS95

**CHALLENGE:** Be strong and take heart, all you who hope in the LORD. *Psalms 31:24* NIV

## ഌ JULY 15 ‿

*Memory Verse 14*

**PROMISE:** The LORD is good to those who wait for Him, To the soul who seeks Him. ²⁶It is good that one should hope and wait quietly For the salvation of the LORD. *Lamentations 3:25–26* NKJV

**PRAYER:** Behold, God is my salvation; I will trust, and not be afraid: for the LORD JEHOVAH is my strength and my song; he also is become my salvation. *Isaiah 12:2* KJV

**CHALLENGE:** You should have the same attitude toward one another that Christ Jesus had, ⁶who though he existed in the form of God did not regard equality with God as something to be grasped, ⁷but emptied himself by taking on the form of a slave, by looking like other men, and by sharing in human nature. ⁸He humbled himself, by becoming obedient to the point of death—even death on a cross! ⁹As a result God exalted him and gave him the name that is above every name, ¹⁰so that at the name of Jesus every knee will bow—in heaven and on earth and under the earth—¹¹and every tongue confess that Jesus Christ is Lord to the glory of God the Father. *Philippians 2:5–11* NET

## ഌ JULY 16 ‿

*Memory Verse 14*

**PROMISE:** But God, being rich in mercy, because of His great love with which He loved us, ⁵even when we were dead in our transgressions, made us alive together with Christ (by grace you have been saved), ⁶and raised us up with Him, and seated us with Him in the heavenly places in Christ Jesus, ⁷so that in the ages to come He might show the surpassing riches of His grace in kindness toward us in Christ Jesus. *Ephesians 2:4–7* NAS95

**PRAYER:** And Hezekiah prayed this prayer before the LORD: "O LORD, God of Israel, you are enthroned between the mighty cherubim! You alone are God of all the kingdoms of the earth. You alone created the heavens and the earth. *2 Kings 19:15* NLT

**CHALLENGE:** The one who oppresses the poor person insults his Maker, but one who is kind to the needy honors Him. *Proverbs 14:31* HCSB

## ᔕᎧ JULY **17** ᏕᎧ

### *Memory Verse 14*

**PROMISE:** "The LORD brings death and makes alive; he brings down to the grave and raises up. ⁷The LORD sends poverty and wealth; he humbles and he exalts. ⁸He raises the poor from the dust and lifts the needy from the ash heap; he seats them with princes and has them inherit a throne of honor. "For the foundations of the earth are the LORD's; upon them he has set the world. *1 Samuel 2:6–8* NIV

**PRAYER:** Though the LORD is on high, Yet He regards the lowly; But the proud He knows from afar. ⁷Though I walk in the midst of trouble, You will revive me; You will stretch out Your hand Against the wrath of my enemies, And Your right hand will save me. *Psalms 138:6–7* NKJV

**CHALLENGE:** Don't let anyone think less of you because you are young. Be an example to all believers in what you say, in the way you live, in your love, your faith, and your purity. *1 Timothy 4:12* NLT

## ᔕᎧ JULY **18** ᏕᎧ

### *Memory Verse 15*

**PROMISE:** Your throne, O God, is forever and ever; A scepter of uprightness is the scepter of Your kingdom. ⁷You have loved righteousness and hated wickedness; Therefore God, Your God, has anointed You With the oil of joy above Your fellows. *Psalms 45:6–7* NAS95

**PRAYER:** O LORD, God of Israel, there is no God like you in all of heaven and earth. You keep your covenant and show unfailing love to all who walk before you in wholehearted devotion. You have kept your promise to your servant David, my father. You made that promise with your own mouth, and with your own hands you have fulfilled it today. *2 Chronicles 6:15* NLT

**CHALLENGE:** And He said to him, "Why are you asking Me about what is good? There is only One who is good; but if you wish to enter into life, keep the commandments." *Matthew 19:17* NAS95

## ℰ JULY 19 ℛ

*Memory Verse 15*

**PROMISE:** And God will generously provide all you need. Then you will always have everything you need and plenty left over to share with others. ⁹As the Scriptures say, "They share freely and give generously to the poor. Their good deeds will be remembered forever." *2 Corinthians 9:8–9* NLT

**PRAYER:** The LORD is exalted over all the nations, his glory above the heavens. ⁵Who is like the LORD our God, the One who sits enthroned on high, ⁶who stoops down to look on the heavens and the earth? *Psalms 113:4–6* NIV

**CHALLENGE:** But he said to her, "You speak as one of the foolish women speaks. Shall we indeed accept good from God, and shall we not accept adversity?" In all this Job did not sin with his lips. *Job 2:10* NKJV

## ℰ JULY 20 ℛ

*Memory Verse 15*

**PROMISE:** Whoever walks in integrity walks securely, but he who makes his ways crooked will be found out. *Proverbs 10:9* ESV

**PRAYER:** For he will deliver the needy when he cries for help, The afflicted also, and him who has no helper. ¹³He will have compassion on the poor and needy, And the lives of the needy he will save. *Psalms 72:12–13* NAS95

**CHALLENGE:** ⁷"You shall not misuse the name of the LORD your God, for the LORD will not hold anyone guiltless who misuses his name. *Exodus 20:6–7* NIV

## ℰℴ JULY 21 ℭℜ

### *Memory Verse 15*

**PROMISE:** He who walks righteously and speaks with sincerity, He who rejects unjust gain And shakes his hands so that they hold no bribe; He who stops his ears from hearing about bloodshed And shuts his eyes from looking upon evil; ¹⁶He will dwell on the heights, His refuge will be the impregnable rock; His bread will be given him, His water will be sure. *Isaiah 33:15–16* NAS95

**PRAYER:** Since you are my rock and my fortress, for the sake of your name lead and guide me. *Psalms 31:3* NIV

**CHALLENGE:** Brothers and sisters, be patient until the Lord comes again. See how farmers wait for their precious crops to grow. They wait patiently for fall and spring rains. ⁸You, too, must be patient. Don't give up hope. The Lord will soon be here. *James 5:7–8* GWORD

## ℰℴ JULY 22 ℭℜ

### *Memory Verse 15*

**PROMISE:** "If only you would prepare your heart and lift up your hands to him in prayer! ¹⁴Get rid of your sins, and leave all iniquity behind you. ¹⁵Then your face will brighten with innocence. You will be strong and free of fear. ¹⁶You will forget your misery; it will be like water flowing away. ¹⁷Your life will be brighter than the noonday. Even darkness will be as bright as morning. ¹⁸Having hope will give you courage. You will be protected and will rest in safety. ¹⁹You will lie down unafraid, and many will look to you for help. *Job 11:13–19* NLT

**PRAYER:** I always thank my God when I pray for you, Philemon, ⁵because I keep hearing about your faith in the Lord Jesus and your love for all of God's people. *Philemon 1:4–5* NLT

**CHALLENGE:** Then Jesus said to them, "Give to Caesar what is Caesar's and to God what is God's." And they were amazed at him. *Mark 12:17* NIV

## ഇ JULY 23 ൨

*Memory Verse 15*

**PROMISE:** Bread gained by deceit is sweet to a man, But afterward his mouth will be filled with gravel. *Proverbs 20:17* NKJV

**PRAYER:** Hannah prayed out loud, "My heart finds joy in the Lord. My head is lifted to the Lord. My mouth mocks my enemies. I rejoice because you saved ‹me›. *1 Samuel 2:1* GWORD

**CHALLENGE:** Through Jesus, therefore, let us continually offer to God a sacrifice of praise—the fruit of lips that confess his name. ¹⁶And do not forget to do good and to share with others, for with such sacrifices God is pleased. *Hebrews 13:15–16* NIV

## ഇ JULY 24 ൨

*Memory Verse 15*

**PROMISE:** The Lord is Israel's king and defender. He is the Lord of Armies. This is what the Lord says: I am the first and the last, and there is no God except me. ⁷If there is anyone like me, let him say so. Let him tell me what happened when I established my people long ago. Then let him predict what will happen to them. *Isaiah 44:6–7* GWORD

**PRAYER:** I wait for the LORD, my soul waits, and in his word I put my hope. ⁶My soul waits for the Lord more than watchmen wait for the morning, more than watchmen wait for the morning. *Psalms 130:5–6* NIV

**CHALLENGE:** Peter said to them, "Repent, and each of you be baptized in the name of Jesus Christ for the forgiveness of your sins; and you will receive the gift of the Holy Spirit. *Acts 2:38* NAS95

## හ JULY 25 ශ

### *Memory Verse 15*

**PROMISE:** The eyes of the LORD are in every place, Watching the evil and the good. *Proverbs 15:3* NAS95

**PRAYER:** The LORD lives! Blessed be my Rock! Let the God of my salvation be exalted. *Psalms 18:46* NKJV

**CHALLENGE:** Dear friends, never take revenge. Leave that to the righteous anger of God. For the Scriptures say, "I will take revenge; I will pay them back," says the LORD. ²⁰Instead, "If your enemies are hungry, feed them. If they are thirsty, give them something to drink. In doing this, you will heap burning coals of shame on their heads." *Romans 12:19–20* NLT

## හ JULY 26 ශ

### *Memory Verse 15*

**PROMISE:** For the word of God is living and effective and sharper than any double-edged sword, penetrating as far as the separation of soul and spirit, joints and marrow. It is able to judge the ideas and thoughts of the heart. ¹³No creature is hidden from Him, but all things are naked and exposed to the eyes of Him to whom we must give an account. *Hebrews 4:12–13* HCSB

**PRAYER:** And He went a little beyond them, and fell on His face and prayed, saying, "My Father, if it is possible, let this cup pass from Me; yet not as I will, but as You will." *Matthew 26:39* NAS95

**CHALLENGE:** Abraham never wavered in believing God's promise. In fact, his faith grew stronger, and in this he brought glory to God. ²¹He was fully convinced that God is able to do whatever he promises. *Romans 4:20–22* NLT

## ℘ JULY 27 ℃

*Memory Verse 15*

**PROMISE:** But the Scriptures declare that we are all prisoners of sin, so we receive God's promise of freedom only by believing in Jesus Christ. *Galatians 3:22* NLT

**PRAYER:** But as for me, I will look to the LORD; I will wait for the God of my salvation; my God will hear me. *Micah 7:7* ESV

**CHALLENGE:** Accept other believers who are weak in faith, and don't argue with them about what they think is right or wrong. ²For instance, one person believes it's all right to eat anything. But another believer with a sensitive conscience will eat only vegetables. *Romans 14:1–2* NLT

## ℘ JULY 28 ℃

*Memory Verse 15*

**PROMISE:** Those who love your law are completely secure; nothing causes them to stumble. *Psalms 119:165* NET

**PRAYER:** After saying all these things, Jesus looked up to heaven and said, "Father, the hour has come. Glorify your Son so he can give glory back to you. ²For you have given him authority over everyone. He gives eternal life to each one you have given him. *John 17:1–2* NLT

**CHALLENGE:** Children, obey your parents because you are Christians. This is the right thing to do. ²"Honor your father and mother ³that everything may go well for you, and you may have a long life on earth." This is an important commandment with a promise. *Ephesians 6:1–3* GWORD

## JULY 29

*Memory Verse 15*

**PROMISE:** Then the kings of the earth, the nobles, the military commanders, the rich, the powerful, and every slave and free person hid in the caves and among the rocks of the mountains. ¹⁶And they said to the mountains and to the rocks, "Fall on us and hide us from the face of the One seated on the throne and from the wrath of the Lamb, ¹⁷because the great day of Their wrath has come! And who is able to stand?" *Revelation 6:15–17* HCSB

**PRAYER:** And even when I am old and gray, O God, do not forsake me, Until I declare Your strength to this generation, Your power to all who are to come. 19 For Your righteousness, O God, reaches to the heavens, You who have done great things; O God, who is like You? *Psalms 71:18–19* NAS95

**CHALLENGE:** For you know what commands we gave you through the Lord Jesus. ³For this is God's will: that you become holy, that you keep away from sexual immorality, ⁴that each of you know how to possess his own body in holiness and honor, ⁵not in lustful passion like the Gentiles who do not know God. *1 Thessalonians 4:2–5* NET

## JULY 30

*Memory Verse 15*

**PROMISE:** For where jealousy and selfish ambition exist, there is disorder and every evil thing. *James 3:16* NAS95

**PRAYER:** "Praise the LORD! For the Lord our God, the Almighty, reigns. ⁷Let us be glad and rejoice, and let us give honor to him. For the time has come for the wedding feast of the Lamb, and his bride has prepared herself. ⁸She has been given the finest of pure white linen to wear." For the fine linen represents the good deeds of God's holy people. *Revelation 19:6–8* NLT

**CHALLENGE:** Observe my days of worship and respect my holy tent. I am the Lord. *Leviticus 19:30* GWORD

# ഇ JULY 31 ഏ

*Memory Verse 15*

**PROMISE:** You murdered Jesus by hanging him on a cross. But the God of our ancestors brought him back to life. ³¹God used his power to give Jesus the highest position as leader and savior. He did this to lead the people of Israel to him, to change the way they think and act, and to forgive their sins. *Acts 5:30–31* GWORD

**PRAYER:** O LORD my God, I take refuge in you; save and deliver me from all who pursue me, ²or they will tear me like a lion and rip me to pieces with no one to rescue me. *Psalms 7:1–2* NIV

**CHALLENGE:** Be angry and do not sin; do not let the sun go down on the cause of your anger. ²⁷Do not give the devil an opportunity. *Ephesians 4:26–27* NET

# August

## ဆာ AUGUST 1 ရ

*Memory Verse 16*

**PROMISE:** The fear of the LORD is the beginning of wisdom; A good understanding have all those who do His commandments; His praise endures forever. *Psalms 111:10* NAS95

**PRAYER:** I will praise You with my whole heart; Before the gods I will sing praises to You. ²I will worship toward Your holy temple, And praise Your name For Your lovingkindness and Your truth; For You have magnified Your word above all Your name. *Psalms 138:1–2* NKJV

**CHALLENGE:** Therefore I do not run like one who runs aimlessly or box like one beating the air. ²⁷Instead, I discipline my body and bring it under strict control, so that after preaching to others, I myself will not be disqualified. *1 Corinthians 9:26–27* HCSB

## ဆာ AUGUST 2 ရ

*Memory Verse 16*

**PROMISE:** Be strong and of good courage, do not fear nor be afraid of them; for the LORD your God, He is the One who goes with you. He will not leave you nor forsake you." *Deuteronomy 31:6* NKJV

**PRAYER:** The Lord GOD will help Me; therefore I have not been humiliated; therefore I have set My face like flint, and I know I will not be put to shame. *Isaiah 50:7* HCSB

**CHALLENGE:** Jesus told them, "If God were your Father, you would love me. After all, I'm here, and I came from God. I didn't come on my own. Instead, God sent me. *John 8:42* GWORD

## ∾ AUGUST 3 ∾

### *Memory Verse 16*

**PROMISE:** How great are His miracles, and how mighty His wonders! His kingdom is an eternal kingdom, and His dominion is from generation to generation. *Daniel 4:3* HCSB

**PRAYER:** You are my hiding place and my shield. I find hope in your word. *Psalms 119:114* NET

**CHALLENGE:** In his grace, God has given us different gifts for doing certain things well. So if God has given you the ability to prophesy, speak out with as much faith as God has given you. ⁷If your gift is serving others, serve them well. If you are a teacher, teach well. ⁸If your gift is to encourage others, be encouraging. If it is giving, give generously. If God has given you leadership ability, take the responsibility seriously. And if you have a gift for showing kindness to others, do it gladly. *Romans 12:6–8* NLT

## ∾ AUGUST 4 ∾

### *Memory Verse 16*

**PROMISE:** Can a woman forget her nursing child, And not have compassion on the son of her womb? Surely they may forget, Yet I will not forget you. *Isaiah 49:15* NKJV

**PRAYER:** For none of us lives to himself, and no one dies to himself. ⁸If we live, we live for the Lord; and if we die, we die for the Lord. Therefore, whether we live or die, we belong to the Lord. *Romans 14:7–8* HCSB

**CHALLENGE:** Tune your ears to wisdom, and concentrate on understanding. ³Cry out for insight, and ask for understanding. ⁴Search for them as you would for silver; seek them like hidden treasures. *Proverbs 2:2–4* NLT

## &) AUGUST 5 (&

*Memory Verse 16*

**PROMISE:** Has not the LORD of Heaven's Armies promised that the wealth of nations will turn to ashes? They work so hard, but all in vain! *Habakkuk 2:13* NLT

**PRAYER:** I thank Christ Jesus our Lord that he has trusted me and has appointed me to do his work with the strength he has given me. *1 Timothy 1:12* GWORD

**CHALLENGE:** "Which ones?" he asked Him. Jesus answered: Do not murder; do not commit adultery; do not steal; do not bear false witness; *Matthew 19:18* HCSB

## &) AUGUST 6 (&

*Memory Verse 16*

**PROMISE:** And you were dead in your trespasses and sins ²in which you previously walked according to the ways of this world, according to the ruler who exercises authority over the lower heavens, the spirit now working in the disobedient. ³We too all previously lived among them in our fleshly desires, carrying out the inclinations of our flesh and thoughts, and we were by nature children under wrath as the others were also. *Ephesians 2:1–3* HCSB

**PRAYER:** But as for me, I will hope continually, And will praise You yet more and more. ¹⁵My mouth shall tell of Your righteousness And of Your salvation all day long; For I do not know the sum of them. *Psalms 71:14–15* NAS95

**CHALLENGE:** The righteous who walks in his integrity—blessed are his children after him! *Proverbs 20:7* ESV

## ᔓ AUGUST 7 ᕤ

*Memory Verse 16*

**PROMISE:** Therefore know that the LORD your God, He is God, the faithful God who keeps covenant and mercy for a thousand generations with those who love Him and keep His commandments *Deuteronomy 7:9* NKJV

**PRAYER:** And I pray this, that your love may abound even more and more in knowledge and every kind of insight ¹⁰so that you can decide what is best, and thus be sincere and blameless for the day of Christ, ¹¹filled with the fruit of righteousness that comes through Jesus Christ to the glory and praise of God. *Philippians 1:9–11* NET

**CHALLENGE:** Cast your cares on the LORD and he will sustain you; he will never let the righteous fall. *Psalms 55:22* NIV

## ᔓ AUGUST 8 ᕤ

*Memory Verse 16*

**PROMISE:** And when He had taken a cup and given thanks, He gave it to them, saying, "Drink from it, all of you; ²⁸for this is My blood of the covenant, which is poured out for many for forgiveness of sins. ²⁹"But I say to you, I will not drink of this fruit of the vine from now on until that day when I drink it new with you in My Father's kingdom." *Matthew 26:27–29* NAS95

**PRAYER:** He was delivered up for our trespasses and raised for our justification. *Romans 4:25* HCSB

**CHALLENGE:** For all who have entered into God's rest have rested from their labors, just as God did after creating the world. ¹¹So let us do our best to enter that rest. But if we disobey God, as the people of Israel did, we will fall. *Hebrews 4:10–11* NLT

## ✠ AUGUST 9 ✠

*Memory Verse 16*

**PROMISE:** You will be made rich in every way so that you can be generous on every occasion, and through us your generosity will result in thanksgiving to God. *2 Corinthians 9:11* NIV

**PRAYER:** This is how God showed his love among us: He sent his one and only Son into the world that we might live through him. ¹⁰This is love: not that we loved God, but that he loved us and sent his Son as an atoning sacrifice for our sins. *1 John 4:9–10* NIV

**CHALLENGE:** If you really fulfill the royal law according to the Scripture, "You shall love your neighbor as yourself," you do well; ⁹but if you show partiality, you commit sin, and are convicted by the law as transgressors. ¹⁰For whoever shall keep the whole law, and yet stumble in one point, he is guilty of all. *James 2:8–10* NKJV

## ✠ AUGUST 10 ✠

*Memory Verse 16*

**PROMISE:** The LORD is like a father to his children, tender and compassionate to those who fear him. ¹⁴For he knows how weak we are; he remembers we are only dust. *Psalms 103:13–14* NLT

**PRAYER:** My aim is to know him, to experience the power of his resurrection, to share in his sufferings, and to be like him in his death, ¹¹and so, somehow, to attain to the resurrection from the dead. ¹²Not that I have already attained this—that is, I have not already been perfected—but I strive to lay hold of that for which Christ Jesus also laid hold of me. *Philippians 3:10–12* NET

**CHALLENGE:** But above all pursue his kingdom and righteousness, and all these things will be given to you as well. *Matthew 6:33* NET

## ഇൗ AUGUST 11 ନ୍ତ

*Memory Verse 16*

**PROMISE:** Hate starts quarrels, but love covers every wrong. *Proverbs 10:12* GWORD

**PRAYER:** Free me from the trap that is set for me, for you are my refuge. ⁵Into your hands I commit my spirit; redeem me, O LORD, the God of truth. *Psalms 31:4–5* NIV

**CHALLENGE:** But as for you, teach what accords with sound doctrine. ²Older men are to be sober-minded, dignified, self-controlled, sound in faith, in love, and in steadfastness. *Titus 2:1–2* ESV

## ഇൗ AUGUST 12 ନ୍ତ

*Memory Verse 16*

**PROMISE:** Then I saw heaven opened, and there was a white horse. Its rider is called Faithful and True, and He judges and makes war in righteousness. ¹²His eyes were like a fiery flame, and many crowns were on His head. He had a name written that no one knows except Himself. ¹³He wore a robe stained with blood, and His name is the Word of God. ¹⁴The armies that were in heaven followed Him on white horses, wearing pure white linen. ¹⁵A sharp sword came from His mouth, so that He might strike the nations with it. He will shepherd them with an iron scepter. He will also trample the winepress of the fierce anger of God, the Almighty. ¹⁶And He has a name written on His robe and on His thigh: KING OF KINGS AND LORD OF LORDS. *Revelation 19:11–16* HCSB

**PRAYER:** Say also: "Save us, O God of our salvation, and gather and deliver us from among the nations, that we may give thanks to your holy name, and glory in your praise. ³⁶Blessed be the LORD, the God of Israel, from everlasting to everlasting!" *1 Chronicles 16:35–36* ESV

**CHALLENGE:** Let us search and try our ways, and turn again to the LORD. *Lamentations 3:40* KJV

## &#8484; AUGUST 13 &#8488;

*Memory Verse 16*

**PROMISE:** God is our refuge and strength, A very present help in trouble. ²Therefore we will not fear, though the earth should change And though the mountains slip into the heart of the sea; ³Though its waters roar and foam, Though the mountains quake at its swelling pride. Selah. *Psalms 46:1–3* NAS95

**PRAYER:** And when you pray, do not keep on babbling like pagans, for they think they will be heard because of their many words. ⁸Do not be like them, for your Father knows what you need before you ask him. *Matthew 6:7–8* NIV

**CHALLENGE:** Never speak harshly to an older man, but appeal to him respectfully as you would to your own father. Talk to younger men as you would to your own brothers. ²Treat older women as you would your mother, and treat younger women with all purity as you would your own sisters. *1 Timothy 5:1–2* NLT

## &#8484; AUGUST 14 &#8488;

*Memory Verse 16*

**PROMISE:** Finishing is better than starting. Patience is better than pride. *Ecclesiastes 7:8* NLT

**PRAYER:** My heart is not proud, O LORD, my eyes are not haughty; I do not concern myself with great matters or things too wonderful for me. *Psalms 131:1* NIV

**CHALLENGE:** Now on the topic of brotherly love you have no need for anyone to write you, for you yourselves are taught by God to love one another. ¹⁰And indeed you are practicing it toward all the brothers and sisters in all of Macedonia. But we urge you, brothers and sisters, to do so more and more, ¹¹to aspire to lead a quiet life, to attend to your own business, and to work with your hands, as we commanded you. ¹²In this way you will live a decent life before outsiders and not be in need. *1 Thessalonians 4:9–12* NET

## ℘ AUGUST 15 ℘

*Memory Verse 17*

**PROMISE:** What can we say about all of this? If God is for us, who can be against us? ³²God didn't spare his own Son but handed him over ‹to death› for all of us. So he will also give us everything along with him. *Romans 8:31–32* GWORD

**PRAYER:** You deserve praise, O LORD! Teach me your statutes! ¹³With my lips I proclaim all the regulations you have revealed. *Psalms 119:12–13* NET

**CHALLENGE:** Since you were brought back to life with Christ, focus on the things that are above—where Christ holds the highest position. ²Keep your mind on things above, not on worldly things. ³You have died, and your life is hidden with Christ in God. *Colossians 3:1–3* GWORD

## ℘ AUGUST 16 ℘

*Memory Verse 17*

**PROMISE:** Then the One seated on the throne said, "Look! I am making everything new." He also said, "Write, because these words are faithful and true." ⁶And He said to me, "It is done! I am the Alpha and the Omega, the Beginning and the End. I will give water as a gift to the thirsty from the spring of life. *Revelation 21:5–6* HCSB

**PRAYER:** I pray that you may be active in sharing your faith, so that you will have a full understanding of every good thing we have in Christ. *Philemon 1:6* NIV

**CHALLENGE:** For I determined to know nothing among you except Jesus Christ, and Him crucified. *1 Corinthians 2:2* NAS95

## ๑ AUGUST 17 ๛

*Memory Verse 17*

**PROMISE:** For though we walk in the flesh, we are not waging war according to the flesh. ⁴For the weapons of our warfare are not of the flesh but have divine power to destroy strongholds. ⁵We destroy arguments and every lofty opinion raised against the knowledge of God, and take every thought captive to obey Christ, ⁶being ready to punish every disobedience, when your obedience is complete. *2 Corinthians 10:3–6* ESV

**PRAYER:** O my God, may your eyes be open and your ears attentive to all the prayers made to you in this place. *2 Chronicles 6:40* NLT

**CHALLENGE:** Timothy, guard what God has entrusted to you. Avoid godless, foolish discussions with those who oppose you with their so-called knowledge. ²¹Some people have wandered from the faith by following such foolishness. May God's grace be with you all. *1 Timothy 6:20–21* NLT

## ๑ AUGUST 18 ๛

*Memory Verse 17*

**PROMISE:** I give them eternal life, and they will never perish. No one can snatch them away from me, ²⁹for my Father has given them to me, and he is more powerful than anyone else. No one can snatch them from the Father's hand. *John 10:28–30* NLT

**PRAYER:** O righteous God, who searches minds and hearts, bring to an end the violence of the wicked and make the righteous secure. *Psalms 7:9* NIV

**CHALLENGE:** But you, why do you criticize your brother? Or you, why do you look down on your brother? For we will all stand before the tribunal of God. ¹¹For it is written: As I live, says the Lord, every knee will bow to Me, and every tongue will give praise to God. ¹²So then, each of us will give an account of himself to God. *Romans 14:10–12* HCSB

## ℰᴑ AUGUST 19 ᴑ℧

*Memory Verse 17*

**PROMISE:** Do not forsake wisdom, and she will protect you; love her, and she will watch over you. ⁷Wisdom is supreme; therefore get wisdom. Though it cost all you have, get understanding. ⁸Esteem her, and she will exalt you; embrace her, and she will honor you. ⁹She will set a garland of grace on your head and present you with a crown of splendor." *Proverbs 4:6–9* NIV

**PRAYER:** How great is the love the Father has lavished on us, that we should be called children of God! And that is what we are! The reason the world does not know us is that it did not know him. *1 John 3:1* NIV

**CHALLENGE:** Turn to Me and be saved, all the ends of the earth. For I am God, and there is no other. ²³By Myself I have sworn; Truth has gone from My mouth, a word that will not be revoked: Every knee will bow to Me, every tongue will swear allegiance. ²⁴It will be said to Me: Righteousness and strength is only in the LORD." All who are enraged against Him will come to Him and be put to shame. *Isaiah 45:22–24* HCSB

## ℰᴑ AUGUST 20 ᴑ℧

*Memory Verse 17*

**PROMISE:** God answered, "I will be with you. And this is your sign that I am the one who has sent you: When you have brought the people out of Egypt, you will worship God at this very mountain." *Exodus 3:12* NLT

**PRAYER:** "No one is holy like the LORD, For there is none besides You, Nor is there any rock like our God. *1 Samuel 2:2* NKJV

**CHALLENGE:** Show respect to the elderly, and honor older people. In this way you show respect for your God. I am the Lord. *Leviticus 19:32* GWORD

## ☙ AUGUST 21 ❧

*Memory Verse 17*

**PROMISE:** A good man out of the good treasure of the heart bringeth forth good things: and an evil man out of the evil treasure bringeth forth evil things. *Matthew 12:35* KJV

**PRAYER:** God remembered us when we were down, His love never quits. ²⁴Rescued us from the trampling boot, His love never quits. ²⁵Takes care of everyone in time of need. His love never quits. ²⁶Thank God, who did it all! His love never quits! *Psalms 136:23–26* MESSAGE

**CHALLENGE:** Looking at the man, Jesus felt genuine love for him. "There is still one thing you haven't done," he told him. "Go and sell all your possessions and give the money to the poor, and you will have treasure in heaven. Then come, follow me." *Mark 10:21* NLT

## ☙ AUGUST 22 ❧

*Memory Verse 17*

**PROMISE:** For the LORD grants wisdom! From his mouth come knowledge and understanding. ⁷He grants a treasure of common sense to the honest. He is a shield to those who walk with integrity. *Proverbs 2:6–7* NLT

**PRAYER:** Rejoice not against me, O mine enemy: when I fall, I shall arise; when I sit in darkness, the LORD shall be a light unto me. *Micah 7:8* KJV

**CHALLENGE:** Brothers, consider your calling: Not many are wise from a human perspective, not many powerful, not many of noble birth. ²⁷Instead, God has chosen what is foolish in the world to shame the wise, and God has chosen what is weak in the world to shame the strong. ²⁸God has chosen what is insignificant and despised in the world—what is viewed as nothing—to bring to nothing what is viewed as something, ²⁹so that no one can boast in His presence. *1 Corinthians 1:26–29* HCSB

## ෨ AUGUST 23 ෬

*Memory Verse 17*

**PROMISE:** But he said to me, "My grace is sufficient for you, for my power is made perfect in weakness." Therefore I will boast all the more gladly of my weaknesses, so that the power of Christ may rest upon me. ¹⁰For the sake of Christ, then, I am content with weaknesses, insults, hardships, persecutions, and calamities. For when I am weak, then I am strong. *2 Corinthians 12:9–10* ESV

**PRAYER:** I hope for your deliverance, O LORD, and I obey your commands. ¹⁶⁷I keep your rules; I love them greatly. ¹⁶⁸I keep your precepts and rules, for you are aware of everything I do. *Psalms 119:166–168* NET

**CHALLENGE:** There are six days when you may work, but the seventh day is a Sabbath of rest, a day of sacred assembly. You are not to do any work; wherever you live, it is a Sabbath to the LORD. *Leviticus 23:3* NIV

## ෨ AUGUST 24 ෬

*Memory Verse 17*

**PROMISE:** The LORD approves of those who are good, but he condemns those who plan wickedness. *Proverbs 12:2* NLT

**PRAYER:** And now, O Lord GOD, you are God, and your words are true, and you have promised this good thing to your servant. ²⁹Now therefore may it please you to bless the house of your servant, so that it may continue forever before you. For you, O Lord GOD, have spoken, and with your blessing shall the house of your servant be blessed forever." *2 Samuel 7:28–29* ESV

**CHALLENGE:** Seek the LORD and His strength; Seek His face continually. *1 Chronicles 16:11* NAS95

## ✥ AUGUST 25 ✥

*Memory Verse 17*

**PROMISE:** But mark this: There will be terrible times in the last days. ²People will be lovers of themselves, lovers of money, boastful, proud, abusive, disobedient to their parents, ungrateful, unholy, ³without love, unforgiving, slanderous, without self-control, brutal, not lovers of the good, ⁴treacherous, rash, conceited, lovers of pleasure rather than lovers of God—⁵having a form of godliness but denying its power. Have nothing to do with them. *2 Timothy 3:1–5* NIV

**PRAYER:** Be not far from me, O God; come quickly, O my God, to help me. *Psalms 71:12* NIV

**CHALLENGE:** Always rejoice, ¹⁷constantly pray, ¹⁸in everything give thanks. For this is God's will for you in Christ Jesus. *1 Thessalonians 5:16–18* NET

## ✥ AUGUST 26 ✥

*Memory Verse 17*

**PROMISE:** "So my advice is, leave these men alone. Let them go. If they are planning and doing these things merely on their own, it will soon be overthrown. ³⁹But if it is from God, you will not be able to overthrow them. You may even find yourselves fighting against God!" *Acts 5:38–39* NLT

**PRAYER:** And they cried out in a loud voice: Salvation belongs to our God, who is seated on the throne, and to the Lamb! *Revelation 7:10* HCSB

**CHALLENGE:** Preach the Word; be prepared in season and out of season; correct, rebuke and encourage—with great patience and careful instruction. *2 Timothy 4:2* NIV

## ✂ AUGUST **27** ✂

*Memory Verse 17*

**PROMISE:** The fear of the LORD leads to life: Then one rests content, untouched by trouble. *Proverbs 19:23* NIV

**PRAYER:** I collapse from grief. Sustain me by your word! ²⁹Remove me from the path of deceit! Graciously give me your law! *Psalms 119:28–29* NET

**CHALLENGE:** Fathers, don't make your children bitter about life. Instead, bring them up in Christian discipline and instruction. *Ephesians 6:4* GWORD

## ✂ AUGUST **28** ✂

*Memory Verse 17*

**PROMISE:** With You I can attack a barrier, and with my God I can leap over a wall. ³⁰God—His way is perfect; the word of the LORD is pure. He is a shield to all who take refuge in Him. *Psalms 18:29–30* HCSB

**PRAYER:** Devote yourselves to prayer, keeping alert in it with an attitude of thanksgiving; ³praying at the same time for us as well, that God will open up to us a door for the word, so that we may speak forth the mystery of Christ, for which I have also been imprisoned. *Colossians 4:2–3* NAS95

**CHALLENGE:** Therefore we must not pass judgment on one another, but rather determine never to place an obstacle or a trap before a brother or sister. *Romans 14:13–14* NET

## ℰℬ AUGUST 29 ℭℜ

*Memory Verse 18*

**PROMISE:** As Jesus was about to go up to Jerusalem, He took the twelve disciples aside by themselves, and on the way He said to them, ¹⁸"Behold, we are going up to Jerusalem; and the Son of Man will be delivered to the chief priests and scribes, and they will condemn Him to death, ¹⁹and will hand Him over to the Gentiles to mock and scourge and crucify Him, and on the third day He will be raised up." *Matthew 20:17–19* NAS95

**PRAYER:** Bless the LORD, O my soul! O LORD my God, You are very great; You are clothed with splendor and majesty, ²Covering Yourself with light as with a cloak, Stretching out heaven like a tent curtain. *Psalms 104:1–2* NAS95

**CHALLENGE:** Stop judging, and you will never be judged. Stop condemning, and you will never be condemned. Forgive, and you will be forgiven. ³⁸Give, and you will receive. A large quantity, pressed together, shaken down, and running over will be put into your pocket. The standards you use for others will be applied to you." *Luke 6:37–38* GWORD

## ℰℬ AUGUST 30 ℭℜ

*Memory Verse 18*

**PROMISE:** On the lips of him who has understanding, wisdom is found, but a rod is for the back of him who lacks sense. ¹⁴The wise lay up knowledge, but the mouth of a fool brings ruin near. *Proverbs 10:13–14* ESV

**PRAYER:** Blessed are the people who know how to praise you. They walk in the light of your presence, O Lord. ¹⁶They find joy in your name all day long. They are joyful in your righteousness ¹⁷because you are the glory of their strength. By your favor you give us victory. *Psalms 89:15–17* GWORD

**CHALLENGE:** The one who steals must steal no longer; rather he must labor, doing good with his own hands, so that he may have something to share with the one who has need. *Ephesians 4:28* NET

## ☙ AUGUST 31 ☙

*Memory Verse 18*

**PROMISE:** I look up toward the hills. From where does my help come? ²My help comes from the LORD, the Creator of heaven and earth! *Psalms 121:1–2* NET

**PRAYER:** Therefore, since we have been declared righteous by faith, we have peace with God through our Lord Jesus Christ. ²We have also obtained access through Him by faith into this grace in which we stand, and we rejoice in the hope of the glory of God. ³And not only that, but we also rejoice in our afflictions, because we know that affliction produces endurance, ⁴endurance produces proven character, and proven character produces hope. ⁵This hope will not disappoint us, because God's love has been poured out in our hearts through the Holy Spirit who was given to us. *Romans 5:1–5* HCSB

**CHALLENGE:** Let us therefore follow after the things which make for peace, and things wherewith one may edify another. *Romans 14:19* KJV

# September

## ∞ SEPTEMBER 1 ∞

*Memory Verse 18*

**PROMISE:** "For I the LORD do not change; therefore you, O children of Jacob, are not consumed. ⁷From the days of your fathers you have turned aside from my statutes and have not kept them. Return to me, and I will return to you, says the LORD of hosts. *Malachi 3:6–7* ESV

**PRAYER:** In his distress he sought the favor of the LORD his God and humbled himself greatly before the God of his fathers. ¹³And when he prayed to him, the LORD was moved by his entreaty and listened to his plea; so he brought him back to Jerusalem and to his kingdom. Then Manasseh knew that the LORD is God. *2 Chronicles 33:12–13* NIV

**CHALLENGE:** So if you consider me your partner, receive him as you would receive me. ¹⁸If he has wronged you at all, or owes you anything, charge that to my account. *Philemon 1:17–18* ESV

## ∞ SEPTEMBER 2 ∞

*Memory Verse 18*

**PROMISE:** A godly life brings huge profits to people who are content with what they have. ⁷We didn't bring anything into the world, and we can't take anything out of it. ⁸As long as we have food and clothes, we should be satisfied. *1 Timothy 6:6–8* GWORD

**PRAYER:** I made the earth, and created man on it. It was My hands that stretched out the heavens, and I commanded all their host. ¹³I have raised him up in righteousness, and will level all roads for him. He will rebuild My city, and set My exiles free, not for a price or a bribe," says the LORD of Hosts. *Isaiah 45:12–13* HCSB

**CHALLENGE:** See to it, brothers and sisters, that none of you has an evil, unbelieving heart that forsakes the living God. [13]But exhort one another each day, as long as it is called "Today," that none of you may become hardened by sin's deception. [14]For we have become partners with Christ, if in fact we hold our initial confidence firm until the end. *Hebrews 3:12–14* NET

## ℰↃ SEPTEMBER 3 ℭↄ

*Memory Verse 18*

**PROMISE:** For God did not destine us for wrath but for gaining salvation through our Lord Jesus Christ. [10]He died for us so that whether we are alert or asleep we will come to life together with him. *1 Thessalonians 5:9–10* NET

**PRAYER:** I am determined to obey your statutes at all times, to the very end. *Psalms 119:112* NET

**CHALLENGE:** [9]But avoid foolish controversies, genealogies, dissensions, and quarrels about the law, for they are unprofitable and worthless. [10]As for a person who stirs up division, after warning him once and then twice, have nothing more to do with him, [11]knowing that such a person is warped and sinful; he is self-condemned. *Titus 3:8–11* ESV

## ℰↃ SEPTEMBER 4 ℭↄ

*Memory Verse 18*

**PROMISE:** But do not overlook this one fact, beloved, that with the Lord one day is as a thousand years, and a thousand years as one day. [9]The Lord is not slow to fulfill his promise as some count slowness, but is patient toward you, not wishing that any should perish, but that all should reach repentance. [10]But the day of the

Lord will come like a thief, and then the heavens will pass away with a roar, and the heavenly bodies will be burned up and dissolved, and the earth and the works that are done on it will be exposed. *2 Peter 3:8–10* ESV

**PRAYER:** Through Jesus, therefore, let us continually offer to God a sacrifice of praise—the fruit of lips that confess his name. *Hebrews 13:15* NIV

**CHALLENGE:** Control your temper, for anger labels you a fool. *Ecclesiastes 7:9* NLT

## ℰ SEPTEMBER 5 ℛ

### *Memory Verse 18*

**PROMISE:** Then I saw an angel coming down from heaven with the key to the abyss and a great chain in his hand. ²He seized the dragon, that ancient serpent who is the Devil and Satan, and bound him for 1,000 years. ³He threw him into the abyss, closed it, and put a seal on it so that he would no longer deceive the nations until the 1,000 years were completed. After that, he must be released for a short time. *Revelation 20:1–3* HCSB

**PRAYER:** By You I have been sustained from my birth; You are He who took me from my mother's womb; My praise is continually of You. ⁷I have become a marvel to many, For You are my strong refuge. *Psalms 71:6–7* NAS95

**CHALLENGE:** What shall we say then? Are we to continue in sin that grace may abound? ²By no means! How can we who died to sin still live in it? *Romans 6:1–2* ESV

## ℰ SEPTEMBER 6 ℛ

### *Memory Verse 18*

**PROMISE:** I asked the Lord three times about this, that it would depart from me. ⁹But he said to me, "My grace is enough for you, for my power is made perfect in weakness." So then, I will boast most gladly about my weaknesses, so that the power of Christ may reside in me. ¹⁰Therefore I am content with weaknesses, with insults, with troubles, with persecutions and difficulties for the sake of Christ, for whenever I am weak, then I am strong. *2 Corinthians 12:8–10* NET

**PRAYER:** Beloved, I pray that all may go well with you and that you may be in good health, as it goes well with your soul. *3 John 1:2* ESV

**CHALLENGE:** Dear friends, since God so loved us, we also ought to love one another. ¹²No one has ever seen God; but if we love one another, God lives in us and his love is made complete in us. *1 John 4:11–12* NIV

## ℅ SEPTEMBER 7 ℃

*Memory Verse 18*

**PROMISE:** My dear brothers and sisters, don't be fooled. ¹⁷Every good present and every perfect gift comes from above, from the Father who made the sun, moon, and stars. The Father doesn't change like the shifting shadows produced by the sun and the moon. *James 1:16–17* GWORD

**PRAYER:** To Him who alone does great wonders, For His lovingkindness is everlasting; ⁵To Him who made the heavens with skill, For His lovingkindness is everlasting; ⁶To Him who spread out the earth above the waters, For His lovingkindness is everlasting; ⁷To Him who made the great lights, For His lovingkindness is everlasting. *Psalms 136:4–7* NAS95

**CHALLENGE:** "You shall not covet your neighbor's house. You shall not covet your neighbor's wife, or his manservant or maidservant, his ox or donkey, or anything that belongs to your neighbor." *Exodus 20:17* NIV

## ℘ SEPTEMBER 8 ℂℛ

*Memory Verse 18*

**PROMISE:** Your word is a lamp to walk by, and a light to illumine my path. *Psalms 119:105* NET

**PRAYER:** Who is a God like You, Pardoning iniquity And passing over the transgression of the remnant of His heritage? He does not retain His anger forever, Because He delights in mercy. ¹⁹He will again have compassion on us, And will subdue our iniquities. You will cast all our sins Into the depths of the sea. *Micah 7:18–19* NKJV

**CHALLENGE:** Above all else, guard your heart, for it is the wellspring of life. *Proverbs 4:23* NIV

## ℘ SEPTEMBER 9 ℂℛ

*Memory Verse 18*

**PROMISE:** The sun will not harm you by day, or the moon by night. ⁷The LORD will protect you from all harm; he will protect your life. ⁸The LORD will protect you in all you do, now and forevermore. *Psalms 121:6–8* NET

**PRAYER:** For as the heavens are higher than the earth, so are my ways higher than your ways, and my thoughts than your thoughts. *Isaiah 55:9* KJV

**CHALLENGE:** We should help others do what is right and build them up in the Lord. ³For even Christ didn't live to please himself. As the Scriptures say, "The insults of those who insult you, O God, have fallen on me." ⁴Such things were written in the Scriptures long ago to teach us. And the Scriptures give us hope and encouragement as we wait patiently for God's promises to be fulfilled. *Romans 15:2–4* NLT

## ∞ SEPTEMBER 10 ∞

*Memory Verse 18*

**PROMISE:** The LORD of hosts is with us; The God of Jacob is our stronghold. Selah. *Psalms 46:7* NAS95

**PRAYER:** And he said, The LORD is my rock, and my fortress, and my deliverer; ³The God of my rock; in him will I trust: he is my shield, and the horn of my salvation, my high tower, and my refuge, my saviour; thou savest me from violence. *2 Samuel 22:2–3* KJV

**CHALLENGE:** You must let no unwholesome word come out of your mouth, but only what is beneficial for the building up of the one in need, that it may give grace to those who hear. ³⁰And do not grieve the Holy Spirit of God, by whom you were sealed for the day of redemption. *Ephesians 4:29–30* NET

## ∞ SEPTEMBER 11 ∞

*Memory Verse 18*

**PROMISE:** God is not unjust; he will not forget your work and the love you have shown him as you have helped his people and continue to help them. *Hebrews 6:10* NIV

**PRAYER:** Where can I go to escape your spirit? Where can I flee to escape your presence? ⁸If I were to ascend to heaven, you would be there. If I were to sprawl out in Sheol, there you would be. ⁹If I were to fly away on the wings of the dawn, and settle down on the other side of the sea, ¹⁰even there your hand would guide me, your right hand would grab hold of me. *Psalms 139:7–10* NET

**CHALLENGE:** Serve eagerly as if you were serving your heavenly master and not merely serving human masters. ⁸You know that your heavenly master will reward all of us for whatever good we do, whether we're slaves or free people. *Ephesians 6:7–8* GWORD

## ℰ SEPTEMBER 12 ℚ

*Memory Verse 19*

**PROMISE:** You come near when I call on You; You say: "Do not be afraid." ⁵⁸Resh You defend my cause, Lord; You redeem my life. *Lamentations 3:57–58* HCSB

**PRAYER:** My shield is God Most High, who saves the upright in heart. *Psalms 7:10* NIV

**CHALLENGE:** Those who love their lives will destroy them, and those who hate their lives in this world will guard them for everlasting life. ²⁶Those who serve me must follow me. My servants will be with me wherever I will be. If people serve me, the Father will honor them. *John 12:25–26* GWORD

## ℰ SEPTEMBER 13 ℚ

*Memory Verse 19*

**PROMISE:** He who keeps instruction is in the way of life, But he who refuses correction goes astray. *Proverbs 10:17* NKJV

**PRAYER:** But God proves His own love for us in that while we were still sinners, Christ died for us! *Romans 5:8* HCSB

**CHALLENGE:** After all, they went on their trip to serve the one named Christ, and they didn't accept any help from the people to whom they went. ⁸We must support believers who go on trips like this so that we can work together with them in spreading the truth. *3 John 1:7–8* GWORD

## ഇ SEPTEMBER 14 ന

*Memory Verse 19*

**PROMISE:** "Talk no more so very proudly; Let no arrogance come from your mouth, For the LORD is the God of knowledge; And by Him actions are weighed. *1 Samuel 2:3* NKJV

**PRAYER:** O LORD, how many are Your works! In wisdom You have made them all; The earth is full of Your possessions. *Psalms 104:24* NAS95

**CHALLENGE:** "What good is an idol carved by man, or a cast image that deceives you? How foolish to trust in your own creation—a god that can't even talk! ¹⁹What sorrow awaits you who say to wooden idols, 'Wake up and save us!' To speechless stone images you say, 'Rise up and teach us!' Can an idol tell you what to do? They may be overlaid with gold and silver, but they are lifeless inside. ²⁰But the LORD is in his holy Temple. Let all the earth be silent before him." *Habakkuk 2:18–20* NLT

## ഇ SEPTEMBER 15 ന

*Memory Verse 19*

**PROMISE:** Looking at them, Jesus said, "With men it is impossible, but not with God, because all things are possible with God." *Mark 10:27* HCSB

**PRAYER:** I will be glad and rejoice in your love, for you saw my affliction and knew the anguish of my soul. ⁸You have not handed me over to the enemy but have set my feet in a spacious place. *Psalms 31:7–8* NIV

**CHALLENGE:** My brethren, do not hold the faith of our Lord Jesus Christ, the Lord of glory, with partiality. ²For if there should come into your assembly a man with gold rings, in fine apparel, and there should also come in a poor man in filthy clothes, ³and you pay attention to the one wearing the fine clothes and say to him, "You sit here in a good place," and say to the poor man, "You stand there," or, "Sit here at my footstool," ⁴have you not shown partiality among yourselves, and become judges with evil thoughts? *James 2:1–4* NKJV

## ᏑᎧ SEPTEMBER 16 ᎧᏒ

*Memory Verse 19*

**PROMISE:** Wickedness never brings stability, but the godly have deep roots. *Proverbs 12:3* NLT

**PRAYER:** "This, then, is how you should pray: "'Our Father in heaven, hallowed be your name, ¹⁰your kingdom come, your will be done on earth as it is in heaven. ¹¹Give us today our daily bread. ¹²Forgive us our debts, as we also have forgiven our debtors. ¹³And lead us not into temptation, but deliver us from the evil one.' ¹⁴For if you forgive men when they sin against you, your heavenly Father will also forgive you. ¹⁵But if you do not forgive men their sins, your Father will not forgive your sins. *Matthew 6:9–15* NIV

**CHALLENGE:** If possible, so far as it depends on you, be at peace with all men. *Romans 12:18* NAS95

## ᏑᎧ SEPTEMBER 17 ᎧᏒ ᎧᏒ

*Memory Verse 19*

**PROMISE:** But I say to you that for every idle word men may speak, they will give account of it in the day of judgment. ³⁷For by your words you will be justified, and by your words you will be condemned." *Matthew 12:36–37* NKJV

**PRAYER:** Be a rock of refuge for me, where I can always go. Give the command to save me, for You are my rock and fortress. ⁴Deliver me, my God, from the power of the wicked, from the grasp of the unjust and oppressive. ⁵For You are my hope, Lord GOD, my confidence from my youth. *Psalms 71:3–5* HCSB

**CHALLENGE:** Likewise, urge the younger men to be self-controlled. ⁷Show yourself in all respects to be a model of good works, and in your teaching show integrity, dignity, ⁸and sound speech that cannot be condemned, so that an opponent may be put to shame, having nothing evil to say about us. *Titus 2:6–8* ESV

## ᔕᔓ SEPTEMBER **18** ᘗᘘ

*Memory Verse 19*

**PROMISE:** After this, the word of the LORD came to Abram in a vision: "Do not be afraid, Abram. I am your shield, your very great reward." *Genesis 15:1* NIV

**PRAYER:** But I have stilled and quieted my soul; like a weaned child with its mother, like a weaned child is my soul within me. ³O Israel, put your hope in the LORD both now and forevermore. *Psalms 131:2–3* NIV

**CHALLENGE:** Love sincerely. Hate evil. Hold on to what is good. ¹⁰Be devoted to each other like a loving family. Excel in showing respect for each other. ¹¹Don't be lazy in showing your devotion. Use your energy to serve the Lord. *Romans 12:9–11* GWORD

## ᔕᔓ SEPTEMBER **19** ᘗᘘ

*Memory Verse 19*

**PROMISE:** For the message of the cross is foolishness to those who are perishing, but it is God's power to us who are being saved. *1 Corinthians 1:18–19* HCSB

**PRAYER:** They sang, "Amen! Blessing and glory and wisdom and thanksgiving and honor and power and strength belong to our God forever and ever! Amen." *Revelation 7:12* NLT

**CHALLENGE:** "Now, therefore," says the LORD, "Turn to Me with all your heart, With fasting, with weeping, and with mourning." ¹³So rend your heart, and not your garments; Return to the LORD your God, For He is gracious and merciful, Slow to anger, and of great kindness; And He relents from doing harm. *Joel 2:12–13* NKJV

## ᏺ SEPTEMBER **20** ᏹ

*Memory Verse 19*

**PROMISE:** Yes, and everyone who wants to live a godly life in Christ Jesus will suffer persecution. ¹³But evil people and impostors will flourish. They will deceive others and will themselves be deceived. *2 Timothy 3:12–13* NLT

**PRAYER:** Then the women said to Naomi, "Blessed be the LORD, who has not left you this day without a close relative; and may his name be famous in Israel! ¹⁵And may he be to you a restorer of life and a nourisher of your old age; for your daughter-in-law, who loves you, who is better to you than seven sons, has borne him." *Ruth 4:14–15* NKJV

**CHALLENGE:** Then he said to them all: "If anyone would come after me, he must deny himself and take up his cross daily and follow me. *Luke 9:23* NIV

## ᏺ SEPTEMBER **21** ᏹ

*Memory Verse 19*

**PROMISE:** The LORD said to him, "Who has made man's mouth? Or who makes him mute or deaf, or seeing or blind? Is it not I, the LORD? ¹²"Now then go, and I, even I, will be with your mouth, and teach you what you are to say." *Exodus 4:11–12* NAS95

**PRAYER:** Show us favor, O LORD, show us favor! For we have had our fill of humiliation, and then some. ⁴We have had our fill of the taunts of the self-assured, of the contempt of the proud. *Psalms 123:3–4* NET

**CHALLENGE:** When the ten others heard about this, they lost their tempers, thoroughly disgusted with the two brothers. ²⁵So Jesus got them together to settle things down. He said, "You've observed how godless rulers throw their weight around, how quickly a little power goes to their heads. ²⁶It's not going to be that way with you. Whoever wants to be great must become a servant. ²⁷Whoever wants to be first among you must be your slave. ²⁸That is what the Son of Man has done: He came to serve, not be served—and then to give away his life in exchange for the many who are held hostage." *Matthew 20:24–28* MESSAGE

## ❧ SEPTEMBER 22 ❧

*Memory Verse 19*

**PROMISE:** "I am the Alpha and the Omega," says the Lord God, "who is and who was and who is to come, the Almighty." *Revelation 1:8* NAS95

**PRAYER:** As they stoned him, Stephen prayed, "Lord Jesus, receive my spirit." ⁶⁰He fell to his knees, shouting, "Lord, don't charge them with this sin!" And with that, he died. *Acts 7:59–60* NLT

**CHALLENGE:** Be still, and know that I am God; I will be exalted among the nations, I will be exalted in the earth! ¹¹The LORD of hosts is with us; The God of Jacob is our refuge. Selah *Psalms 46:10–11* NKJV

## ❧ SEPTEMBER 23 ❧

*Memory Verse 19*

**PROMISE:** But we are looking forward to the new heavens and new earth he has promised, a world filled with God's righteousness. *2 Peter 3:13* NLT

**PRAYER:** And they sang together by course in praising and giving thanks unto the LORD; because he is good, for his mercy endureth for ever toward Israel. And all the people shouted with a great shout, when they praised the LORD, because the foundation of the house of the LORD was laid. *Ezra 3:11* KJV

**CHALLENGE:** You must put away every kind of bitterness, anger, wrath, quarreling, and evil, slanderous talk. ³²Instead, be kind to one another, compassionate, forgiving one another, just as God in Christ also forgave you. *Ephesians 4:31–32* NET

## ❧ SEPTEMBER 24 ❧

*Memory Verse 19*

**PROMISE:** I have told you all this so that you may have peace in me. Here on earth you will have many trials and sorrows. But take heart, because I have overcome the world." *John 16:33* NLT

**PRAYER:** I rejoice in the lifestyle prescribed by your rules as if they were riches of all kinds. *Psalms 119:14* NET

**CHALLENGE:** And Jesus answering saith unto them, Have faith in God. *Mark 11:22* KJV

## ❧ SEPTEMBER 25 ❧

*Memory Verse 19*

**PROMISE:** Christ is your life. When he appears, then you, too, will appear with him in glory. *Colossians 3:4* GWORD

**PRAYER:** Brothers and sisters, I do not consider myself to have attained this. Instead I am single-minded: Forgetting the things that are behind and reaching out for the things that are ahead, ¹⁴with this goal in mind, I strive toward the prize of the upward call of God in Christ Jesus. ¹⁵Therefore let those of us who are "perfect" embrace this point of view. If you think otherwise, God will reveal to you the error of your ways. ¹⁶Nevertheless, let us live up to the standard that we have already attained. *Philippians 3:13–16* NET

**CHALLENGE:** If your boss is angry at you, don't quit! A quiet spirit can overcome even great mistakes. *Ecclesiastes 10:4* NLT

## ❧ SEPTEMBER 26 ❧

*Memory Verse 20*

**PROMISE:** Remember the things I have done in the past. For I alone am God! I am God, and there is none like me. ¹⁰Only I can tell you the future before it even happens. Everything I plan will come to pass, for I do whatever I wish. *Isaiah 46:9–10* NLT

**PRAYER:** I will call on the LORD, who is worthy to be praised: so shall I be saved from mine enemies. *2 Samuel 22:4* KJV

**CHALLENGE:** "Do not store up for yourselves treasures on earth, where moth and rust destroy, and where thieves break in and steal. ²⁰But store up for yourselves treasures in heaven, where moth and rust do not destroy, and where thieves do not break in and steal. ²¹For where your treasure is, there your heart will be also. *Matthew 6:19–21* NIV

## ๕๏ SEPTEMBER 27 ๏ง

*Memory Verse 20*

**PROMISE:** For thus says the LORD of hosts: Yet once more, in a little while, I will shake the heavens and the earth and the sea and the dry land. ⁷And I will shake all nations, so that the treasures of all nations shall come in, and I will fill this house with glory, says the LORD of hosts. ⁸The silver is mine, and the gold is mine, declares the LORD of hosts. *Haggai 2:6–8* ESV

**PRAYER:** And the LORD, He is the One who goes before you. He will be with you, He will not leave you nor forsake you; do not fear nor be dismayed." *Deuteronomy 31:8* NKJV

**CHALLENGE:** Thieves are jealous of each other's loot, but the godly are well rooted and bear their own fruit. *Proverbs 12:12* NLT

## ๕๏ SEPTEMBER 28 ๏ง

*Memory Verse 20*

**PROMISE:** But at the end of those days, I, Nebuchadnezzar, looked up to heaven, and my sanity returned to me. Then I praised the Most High and honored and glorified Him who lives forever: For His dominion is an everlasting dominion, and His kingdom is from generation to generation. [35]All the inhabitants of the earth are counted as nothing, and He does what He wants with the army of heaven and the inhabitants of the earth. There is no one who can hold back His hand or say to Him, "What have You done?" *Daniel 4:34–35* HCSB

**PRAYER:** Now therefore, I pray, if I have found grace in Your sight, show me now Your way, that I may know You and that I may find grace in Your sight. And consider that this nation is Your people." *Exodus 33:13* NKJV

**CHALLENGE:** May God, who gives this patience and encouragement, help you live in complete harmony with each other, as is fitting for followers of Christ Jesus. [6]Then all of you can join together with one voice, giving praise and glory to God, the Father of our Lord Jesus Christ. *Romans 15:5–6* NLT

## ∞ SEPTEMBER 29 ∞

*Memory Verse 20*

**PROMISE:** I guide you in the way of wisdom and lead you along straight paths. [12]When you walk, your steps will not be hampered; when you run, you will not stumble. *Proverbs 4:11–12* NIV

**PRAYER:** Your words are sweeter in my mouth than honey! [104]Your precepts give me discernment. Therefore I hate all deceitful actions. *Psalms 119:103–104* NET

**CHALLENGE:** On the contrary: "If your enemy is hungry, feed him; if he is thirsty, give him something to drink. In doing this, you will heap burning coals on his head." *Romans 12:19–20* NIV

## ∞ SEPTEMBER 30 ∞

*Memory Verse 20*

**PROMISE:** But Jesus knew their thoughts, and said to them: "Every kingdom divided against itself is brought to desolation, and every city or house divided against itself will not stand. *Matthew 12:25* NKJV

**PRAYER:** Let the glory of the LORD endure forever; Let the LORD be glad in His works; [32]He looks at the earth, and it trembles; He touches the mountains, and they smoke. [33]I will sing to the LORD as long as I live; I will sing praise to my God while I have my being. *Psalms 104:31–33* NAS95

**CHALLENGE:** Therefore, be on the alert—for you do not know when the master of the house is coming, whether in the evening, at midnight, or when the rooster crows, or in the morning—[36]in case he should come suddenly and find you asleep. [37]"What I say to you I say to all, 'Be on the alert!'" *Mark 13:35–37* NAS95

# October

## ❧ OCTOBER 1 ☙

*Memory Verse 20*

**PROMISE:** Observe my Sabbaths and have reverence for my sanctuary. I am the LORD. ³"If you follow my decrees and are careful to obey my commands, ⁴I will send you rain in its season, and the ground will yield its crops and the trees of the field their fruit. ⁵Your threshing will continue until grape harvest and the grape harvest will continue until planting, and you will eat all the food you want and live in safety in your land. *Leviticus 26:2–5* NIV

**PRAYER:** I am afflicted and needy; hurry to me, God. You are my help and my deliverer; LORD, do not delay. ¹LORD, I seek refuge in You; let me never be disgraced. ²In Your justice, rescue and deliver me; listen closely to me and save me. *Psalms 70:5–71:2* HCSB

**CHALLENGE:** Now the Lord spoke to Paul in the night by a vision, "Do not be afraid, but speak, and do not keep silent; ¹⁰for I am with you, and no one will attack you to hurt you; for I have many people in this city." *Acts 18:9–10* NKJV

## ❧ OCTOBER 2 ☙

*Memory Verse 20*

**PROMISE:** When words are many, transgression is not lacking, but whoever restrains his lips is prudent. ²⁰The tongue of the righteous is choice silver; the heart of the wicked is of little worth. *Proverbs 10:19–20* ESV

**PRAYER:** For if, while we were enemies, we were reconciled to God through the death of His Son, then how much more, having been reconciled, will we be saved by His life! ¹¹And not only that, but we also rejoice in God through our Lord Jesus Christ. We have now received this reconciliation through Him. *Romans 5:10–11* HCSB

**CHALLENGE:** And Jesus *answered them, saying, "The hour has come for the Son of Man to be glorified. ²⁴"Truly, truly, I say to you, unless a grain of wheat falls into the earth and dies, it remains alone; but if it dies, it bears much fruit. *John 12:23–24* NAS95

## ℘ OCTOBER 3 ℘

*Memory Verse 20*

**PROMISE:** If anyone acknowledges that Jesus is the Son of God, God lives in him and he in God. ¹⁶And so we know and rely on the love God has for us. God is love. Whoever lives in love lives in God, and God in him. ¹⁷In this way, love is made complete among us so that we will have confidence on the day of judgment, because in this world we are like him. *1 John 4:15–17* NIV

**PRAYER:** Jesus used this illustration with his disciples to show them that they need to pray all the time and never give up. *Luke 18:1* GWORD

**CHALLENGE:** But the believers who were scattered preached the Good News about Jesus wherever they went. *Acts 8:4* NLT

## ℘ OCTOBER 4 ℘

*Memory Verse 20*

**PROMISE:** "Yes," Jesus replied, "and I assure you that everyone who has given up house or brothers or sisters or mother or father or children or property, for my sake and for the Good News, ³⁰will receive now in return a hundred times as many houses, brothers, sisters, mothers, children, and property—along with persecution.

And in the world to come that person will have eternal life. ³¹But many who are the greatest now will be least important then, and those who seem least important now will be the greatest then." *Mark 10:29–31* NLT

**PRAYER:** The LORD is exalted, for He dwells on high; He has filled Zion with justice and righteousness. ⁶There will be times of security for you—a storehouse of salvation, wisdom, and knowledge. The fear of the LORD is Zion's treasure. *Isaiah 33:5–6* HCSB

**CHALLENGE:** For I am not ashamed of the gospel of Christ, for it is the power of God to salvation for everyone who believes, for the Jew first and also for the Greek. *Romans 1:16* NKJV

## ℘ OCTOBER 5 ℃

*Memory Verse 20*

**PROMISE:** So you must remain faithful to what you have been taught from the beginning. If you do, you will remain in fellowship with the Son and with the Father. ²⁵And in this fellowship we enjoy the eternal life he promised us. *1 John 2:24–25* NLT

**PRAYER:** If My people who are called by My name will humble themselves, and pray and seek My face, and turn from their wicked ways, then I will hear from heaven, and will forgive their sin and heal their land. *2 Chronicles 7:14* NKJV

**CHALLENGE:** The fact is, even if you remain silent now, someone else will help and rescue the Jews, but you and your relatives will die. And who knows, you may have gained your royal position for a time like this." *Esther 4:14* GWORD

## ℘ OCTOBER 6 ℃

*Memory Verse 20*

**PROMISE:** He guards the paths of the just and protects those who are faithful to him. *Proverbs 2:8* NLT

**PRAYER:** But Abram said, "O Sovereign LORD, what can you give me since I remain childless and the one who will inherit my estate is Eliezer of Damascus?" ³And Abram said, "You have given me no children; so a servant in my household will be my heir." ⁴Then the word of the LORD came to him: "This man will not be your heir, but a son coming from your own body will be your heir." *Genesis 15:2–4* NIV

**CHALLENGE:** "Do for other people everything you want them to do for you. *Luke 6:31* GWORD

## ஐ OCTOBER 7 ଔ

*Memory Verse 20*

**PROMISE:** The Father and I are one." *John 10:30* NLT

**PRAYER:** I collapse in the dirt. Revive me with your word! ²⁶I told you about my ways and you answered me. Teach me your statutes! ²⁷Help me to understand what your precepts mean! Then I can meditate on your marvelous teachings. *Psalms 119:25–27* NET

**CHALLENGE:** Finally, be strong in the Lord and in the strength of his might. ¹¹Put on the whole armor of God, that you may be able to stand against the schemes of the devil. ¹²For we do not wrestle against flesh and blood, but against the rulers, against the authorities, against the cosmic powers over this present darkness, against the spiritual forces of evil in the heavenly places. ¹³Therefore take up the whole armor of God, that you may be able to withstand in the evil day, and having done all, to stand firm. *Ephesians 6:10–13* ESV

## ஐ OCTOBER 8 ଔ

*Memory Verse 20*

**PROMISE:** But people who want to get rich keep falling into temptation. They are trapped by many stupid and harmful desires which drown them in destruction and ruin. ¹⁰Certainly, the love of money is the root of all kinds of evil. Some people who have set their hearts on getting rich have wandered away from the Christian faith and have caused themselves a lot of grief. *1 Timothy 6:9–10* GWORD

**PRAYER:** Yet I will rejoice in the LORD, I will joy in the God of my salvation. *Habakkuk 3:18* NKJV

**CHALLENGE:** Accept one another, then, just as Christ accepted you, in order to bring praise to God. *Romans 15:7–8* NIV

## ೮ OCTOBER 9 ೮౩

### *Memory Verse 20*

**PROMISE:** But cowards, unbelievers, the corrupt, murderers, the immoral, those who practice witchcraft, idol worshipers, and all liars—their fate is in the fiery lake of burning sulfur. This is the second death." *Revelation 21:8* NLT

**PRAYER:** I will praise thee, O LORD, with my whole heart; I will shew forth all thy marvellous works. ²I will be glad and rejoice in thee: I will sing praise to thy name, O thou most High. *Psalms 9:1–2* KJV

**CHALLENGE:** Be happy in your confidence, be patient in trouble, and pray continually. ¹³Share what you have with God's people who are in need. Be hospitable. *Romans 12:12–13* GWORD

## ೮ OCTOBER 10 ೮౩

### *Memory Verse 21*

**PROMISE:** For since he himself suffered when he was tempted, he is able to help those who are tempted. *Hebrews 2:18* NET

**PRAYER:** He delivered me from my strong enemy, From those who hated me; For they were too strong for me. ¹⁹They confronted me in the day of my calamity, But the LORD was my support. *2 Samuel 22:18–19* NKJV

**CHALLENGE:** ⁸But when Simon Peter saw it, he fell down at Jesus' knees, saying, "Depart from me, for I am a sinful man, O Lord." ⁹For he and all who were with him were astonished at the catch of fish that they had taken, ¹⁰and so also were James and John, sons of Zebedee, who were partners with Simon. And Jesus said to Simon, "Do not be afraid; from now on you will be catching men." ¹¹And when they had brought their boats to land, they left everything and followed him. *Luke 5:7–11* ESV

## ∾ OCTOBER 11 ∾

*Memory Verse 21*

**PROMISE:** "No one can serve two masters. Either he will hate the one and love the other, or he will be devoted to the one and despise the other. You cannot serve both God and Money. *Matthew 6:24* NIV

**PRAYER:** Oh, clap your hands, all you peoples! Shout to God with the voice of triumph! ²For the LORD Most High is awesome; He is a great King over all the earth. *Psalms 47:1–2* NKJV

**CHALLENGE:** However, be careful, and watch yourselves closely so that you don't forget the things which you have seen with your own eyes. Don't let them fade from your memory as long as you live. Teach them to your children and grandchildren. *Deuteronomy 4:9* GWORD

## ∾ OCTOBER 12 ∾

*Memory Verse 21*

**PROMISE:** All Scripture is inspired by God and is useful to teach us what is true and to make us realize what is wrong in our lives. It corrects us when we are wrong and teaches us to do what is right. ¹⁷God uses it to prepare and equip his people to do every good work. *2 Timothy 3:16–17* NLT

**PRAYER:** Oh, give thanks to the LORD, for He is good! For His mercy endures forever. ²Oh, give thanks to the God of gods! For His mercy endures forever. ³Oh, give thanks to the Lord of lords! For His mercy endures forever. *Psalms 136:1–3* NKJV

**CHALLENGE:** So be careful to do what the LORD your God has commanded you; do not turn aside to the right or to the left. ³³Walk in all the way that the LORD your God has commanded you, so that you may live and prosper and prolong your days in the land that you will possess. *Deuteronomy 5:32–33* NIV

## ❧ OCTOBER 13 ☙

*Memory Verse 21*

**PROMISE:** All praise to God, the Father of our Lord Jesus Christ. God is our merciful Father and the source of all comfort. ⁴He comforts us in all our troubles so that we can comfort others. When they are troubled, we will be able to give them the same comfort God has given us. *2 Corinthians 1:3–4* NLT

**PRAYER:** May the God of hope fill you with all joy and peace as you trust in him, so that you may overflow with hope by the power of the Holy Spirit. *Romans 15:13* NIV

**CHALLENGE:** Then Jesus said to His disciples, "If anyone desires to come after Me, let him deny himself, and take up his cross, and follow Me. *Matthew 16:24* NKJV

## ❧ OCTOBER 14 ☙

*Memory Verse 21*

**PROMISE:** "The LORD kills and makes alive; He brings down to the grave and brings up. ⁷The LORD makes poor and makes rich; He brings low and lifts up. ⁸He raises the poor from the dust And lifts the beggar from the ash heap, To set them among princes And make them inherit the throne of glory. "For the pillars of the earth are the LORD's, And He has set the world upon them. *1 Samuel 2:6–8* NKJV

**PRAYER:** Agrippa interrupted him. "Do you think you can persuade me to become a Christian so quickly?" ²⁹Paul replied, "Whether quickly or not, I pray to God that both you and everyone here in this audience might become the same as I am, except for these chains." *Acts 26:28–29* NLT

**CHALLENGE:** Jesus knew they were up to no good. He said, "Why are you playing these games with me? Why are you trying to trap me? ¹⁹Do you have a coin? Let me see it." They handed him a silver piece. ²⁰"This engraving—who does it look like? And whose name is on it?" ²¹They said, "Caesar." "Then give Caesar what is his, and give God what is his." ²²The Pharisees were speechless. They went off shaking their heads. *Matthew 22:18–22* MESSAGE

## ❧ OCTOBER 15 ☙

*Memory Verse 21*

**PROMISE:** When I saw him, I fell at his feet as though dead. But he laid his right hand on me, saying, "Fear not, I am the first and the last, ¹⁸and the living one. I died, and behold I am alive forevermore, and I have the keys of Death and Hades. *Revelation 1:17–18* ESV

**PRAYER:** Your name, O LORD, endures forever, Your fame, O LORD, throughout all generations. ¹⁴For the LORD will judge His people, And He will have compassion on His servants. *Psalms 135:13–14* NKJV

**CHALLENGE:** I have discovered this principle of life—that when I want to do what is right, I inevitably do what is wrong. ²²I love God's law with all my heart. ²³But there is another power within me that is at war with my mind. This power makes me a slave to the sin that is still within me. ²⁴Oh, what a miserable person I am! Who will free me from this life that is dominated by sin and death? ²⁵Thank God! The answer is in Jesus Christ our Lord. So you see how it is: In my mind I really want to obey God's law, but because of my sinful nature I am a slave to sin. *Romans 7:21–25* NLT

## ❦ OCTOBER **16** ❧

*Memory Verse 21*

**PROMISE:** Can anything ever separate us from Christ's love? Does it mean he no longer loves us if we have trouble or calamity, or are persecuted, or hungry, or destitute, or in danger, or threatened with death? [36](As the Scriptures say, "For your sake we are killed every day; we are being slaughtered like sheep.") [37]No, despite all these things, overwhelming victory is ours through Christ, who loved us. *Romans 8:35–37* NLT

**PRAYER:** I will give thanks to the LORD because of his righteousness and will sing praise to the name of the LORD Most High. *Psalms 7:17* NIV

**CHALLENGE:** [47]If anyone hears my words and doesn't follow them, I don't condemn them. I didn't come to condemn the world but to save the world. [48]Those who reject me by not accepting what I say have a judge appointed for them. The words that I have spoken will judge them on the last day. *John 12:47–49* GWORD

## ❦ OCTOBER **17** ❧

*Memory Verse 21*

**PROMISE:** The LORD also will be a stronghold for the oppressed, A stronghold in times of trouble; [10]And those who know Your name will put their trust in You, For You, O LORD, have not forsaken those who seek You. *Psalms 9:9–10* NAS95

**PRAYER:** I am the LORD, that is My name; And My glory I will not give to another, Nor My praise to carved images. *Isaiah 42:8* NKJV

**CHALLENGE:** "Woe to the one who argues with his Maker—one clay pot among many. Does clay say to the one forming it, 'What are you making?' Or does your work say, 'He has no hands'? [10]How absurd is the one who says to his father, 'What are you fathering?' or to his mother, 'What are you giving birth to?'" [11]This is what the LORD, the Holy One of Israel and its Maker, says: "Ask Me what is to happen to My sons, and instruct Me about the work of My hands. *Isaiah 45:9–11* HCSB

## ஒ OCTOBER **18** ௧

### *Memory Verse 21*

**PROMISE:** Young people, it's wonderful to be young! Enjoy every minute of it. Do everything you want to do; take it all in. But remember that you must give an account to God for everything you do. *Ecclesiastes 11:9* NLT

**PRAYER:** Let all who seek You rejoice and be glad in You; let those who love Your salvation continually say, "God is great!" *Psalms 70:4* HCSB

**CHALLENGE:** I will meditate on your precepts and focus on your behavior. *Psalms 119:15* NET

## ஒ OCTOBER **19** ௧

### *Memory Verse 21*

**PROMISE:** Never again will they hunger; never again will they thirst. The sun will not beat upon them, nor any scorching heat. ¹⁷For the Lamb at the center of the throne will be their shepherd; he will lead them to springs of living water. And God will wipe away every tear from their eyes." *Revelation 7:16–17* NIV

**PRAYER:** Now I, Nebuchadnezzar, praise, exalt, and glorify the King of heaven, because all His works are true and His ways are just. He is able to humble those who walk in pride. *Daniel 4:37* HCSB

**CHALLENGE:** And now, dear children, continue in him, so that when he appears we may be confident and unashamed before him at his coming. *1 John 2:28* NIV

## 🔊 OCTOBER 20 🔊

*Memory Verse 21*

**PROMISE:** For the grace of God has appeared, bringing salvation for all people, ¹²training us to renounce ungodliness and worldly passions, and to live self-controlled, upright, and godly lives in the present age, ¹³waiting for our blessed hope, the appearing of the glory of our great God and Savior Jesus Christ, ¹⁴who gave himself for us to redeem us from all lawlessness and to purify for himself a people for his own possession who are zealous for good works. *Titus 2:11–14* ESV

**PRAYER:** Be merciful to me, O LORD, for I am in distress; my eyes grow weak with sorrow, my soul and my body with grief. ¹⁰My life is consumed by anguish and my years by groaning; my strength fails because of my affliction, and my bones grow weak. *Psalms 31:9–10* NIV

**CHALLENGE:** Therefore, brothers and sisters, stand firm and hold on to the traditions that we taught you, whether by speech or by letter. *2 Thessalonians 2:15* NET

## 🔊 OCTOBER 21 🔊

*Memory Verse 21*

**PROMISE:** Fear not, O land; Be glad and rejoice, For the LORD has done marvelous things! ²²Do not be afraid, you beasts of the field; For the open pastures are springing up, And the tree bears its fruit; The fig tree and the vine yield their strength. ²³Be glad then, you children of Zion, And rejoice in the LORD your God; For He has given you the former rain faithfully, And He will cause the rain to come down for you—The former rain, And the latter rain in the first month. *Joel 2:21–23* NKJV

**PRAYER:** Let my meditation be pleasing to Him; As for me, I shall be glad in the LORD. *Psalms 104:34* NAS95

**CHALLENGE:** Imitate God, since you are the children he loves. ²Live in love as Christ also loved us. He gave his life for us as an offering and sacrifice, a soothing aroma to God. *Ephesians 5:1–2* GWORD

## ❧ OCTOBER 22 ❧

*Memory Verse 21*

**PROMISE:** The fear of the wicked, it shall come upon him: but the desire of the righteous shall be granted. *Proverbs 10:24* KJV

**PRAYER:** Whatever the LORD pleases He does, In heaven and in earth, In the seas and in all deep places. ⁷He causes the vapors to ascend from the ends of the earth; He makes lightning for the rain; He brings the wind out of His treasuries. *Psalms 135:6–7* NKJV

**CHALLENGE:** Also get rid of your anger, hot tempers, hatred, cursing, obscene language, and all similar sins. ⁹Don't lie to each other. You've gotten rid of the person you used to be and the life you used to live, ¹⁰and you've become a new person. This new person is continually renewed in knowledge to be like its Creator. *Colossians 3:8–10* GWORD

## ❧ OCTOBER 23 ❧

*Memory Verse 21*

**PROMISE:** O LORD, your instructions endure; they stand secure in heaven. ⁹⁰You demonstrate your faithfulness to all generations. You established the earth and it stood firm. ⁹¹Today they stand firm by your decrees, for all things are your servants. *Psalms 119:89–91* NET

**PRAYER:** Dear brothers and sisters, I urge you in the name of our Lord Jesus Christ to join in my struggle by praying to God for me. Do this because of your love for me, given to you by the Holy Spirit. ³¹Pray that I will be rescued from those in Judea who refuse to obey God. Pray also that the believers there will be willing to accept the donation I am taking to Jerusalem. *Romans 15:30–31* NLT

**CHALLENGE:** I will sing of the steadfast love of the LORD, forever; with my mouth I will make known your faithfulness to all generations. *Psalms 89:1* ESV

## ෨ OCTOBER 24 ෫

*Memory Verse 22*

**PROMISE:** But the wisdom from above is first pure, then peaceable, gentle, reasonable, full of mercy and good fruits, unwavering, without hypocrisy. [18]And the seed whose fruit is righteousness is sown in peace by those who make peace. *James 3:17–18* NAS95

**PRAYER:** Sing praises to God, sing praises! Sing praises to our King, sing praises! [7]For God is the King of all the earth; Sing praises with understanding. [8]God reigns over the nations; God sits on His holy throne. *Psalms 47:6–8* NKJV

**CHALLENGE:** Dear friend, never imitate evil, but imitate good. The person who does good is from God. The person who does evil has never seen God. *3 John 1:11* GWORD

## ෨ OCTOBER 25 ෫

*Memory Verse 22*

**PROMISE:** He took him outside and said, "Look up at the heavens and count the stars—if indeed you can count them." Then he said to him, "So shall your offspring be." [6]Abram believed the LORD, and he credited it to him as righteousness. *Genesis 15:5–6* NIV

**PRAYER:** It was at this time that He went off to the mountain to pray, and He spent the whole night in prayer to God. *Luke 6:12* NAS95

**CHALLENGE:** Again I say, rejoice! [5]Let everyone see your gentleness. The Lord is near! *Philippians 4:4–6* NET

## ౭ OCTOBER **26** ౧

*Memory Verse 22*

**PROMISE:** Everyone who believes in him is declared right with God—something the law of Moses could never do. *Acts 13:39* NLT

**PRAYER:** Make haste, O God, to deliver me; make haste to help me, O LORD. *Psalms 70:1* KJV

**CHALLENGE:** But we command you, brothers and sisters, in the name of our Lord Jesus Christ, to keep away from any brother who lives an undisciplined life and not according to the tradition they received from us. *2 Thessalonians 3:6* NET

## ౭ OCTOBER **27** ౧

*Memory Verse 22*

**PROMISE:** He who is kind to the poor lends to the LORD, and he will reward him for what he has done. *Proverbs 19:17* NIV

**PRAYER:** He gives power to the weak and strength to the powerless. ³⁰Even youths will become weak and tired, and young men will fall in exhaustion. ³¹But those who trust in the LORD will find new strength. They will soar high on wings like eagles. They will run and not grow weary. They will walk and not faint. *Isaiah 40:29–31* NLT

**CHALLENGE:** These words I am commanding you today must be kept in mind, ⁷and you must teach them to your children and speak of them as you sit in your house, as you walk along the road, as you lie down, and as you get up. ⁸You should tie them as a reminder on your forearm and fasten them as symbols on your forehead. *Deuteronomy 6:6–8* NET

## ❦ OCTOBER **28** ❧

*Memory Verse 22*

**PROMISE:** The one who is victorious and keeps My works to the end: I will give him authority over the nations—²⁷and he will shepherd them with an iron scepter; he will shatter them like pottery—just as I have received this from My Father. ²⁸I will also give him the morning star. *Revelation 2:26–28* HCSB

**PRAYER:** Let them give glory to the LORD, And declare His praise in the coastlands. ¹³The LORD shall go forth like a mighty man; He shall stir up His zeal like a man of war. He shall cry out, yes, shout aloud; He shall prevail against His enemies. *Isaiah 42:12–13* NKJV

**CHALLENGE:** Never pay back evil for evil to anyone. Respect what is right in the sight of all men. *Romans 12:17* NAS95

## ❦ OCTOBER **29** ❧

*Memory Verse 22*

**PROMISE:** Those who have been delivered will go up on Mount Zion in order to rule over Esau's mountain. Then the LORD will reign as King! *Obadiah 1:21* NET

**PRAYER:** O LORD, our Lord, how majestic is your name in all the earth! You have set your glory above the heavens. ²From the lips of children and infants you have ordained praise because of your enemies, to silence the foe and the avenger. *Psalms 8:1–2* NIV

**CHALLENGE:** Do not let kindness and truth leave you; Bind them around your neck, Write them on the tablet of your heart. ⁴So you will find favor and good repute In the sight of God and man. *Proverbs 3:3–4* NAS95

## ഇ OCTOBER 30 ॐ

*Memory Verse 22*

**PROMISE:** He raises the poor from the dust. He lifts the needy from the trash heap in order to make them sit with nobles and even to make them inherit a glorious throne. "The pillars of the earth are the Lord's. He has set the world on them. [9]He safeguards the steps of his faithful ones, but wicked people are silenced in darkness because humans cannot succeed by their own strength. *1 Samuel 2:8–9* GWORD

**PRAYER:** We have thought on Your lovingkindness, O God, In the midst of Your temple. [10]As is Your name, O God, So is Your praise to the ends of the earth; Your right hand is full of righteousness. *Psalms 48:9–10* NAS95

**CHALLENGE:** For Christ did not send me to baptize, but to evangelize—not with clever words, so that the cross of Christ will not be emptied of its effect. *1 Corinthians 1:17* HCSB

## ഇ OCTOBER 31 ॐ

*Memory Verse 22*

**PROMISE:** You, O LORD, remain forever; Your throne from generation to generation. *Lamentations 5:19* NKJV

**PRAYER:** But there is a place where someone has testified: "What is man that you are mindful of him, the son of man that you care for him? [7]You made him a little lower than the angels; you crowned him with glory and honor [8]and put everything under his feet." In putting everything under him, God left nothing that is not subject to him. Yet at present we do not see everything subject to him. *Hebrews 2:6–8* NIV

**CHALLENGE:** For I have kept the ways of the LORD; I have not turned from my God to follow evil. [23]I have followed all his regulations; I have never abandoned his decrees. [24]I am blameless before God; I have kept myself from sin. *2 Samuel 22:22–24* NLT

# November

## ∞ NOVEMBER 1 ∞

*Memory Verse 22*

**PROMISE:** "Therefore I tell you, do not worry about your life, what you will eat or drink; or about your body, what you will wear. Is not life more important than food, and the body more important than clothes? ²⁶Look at the birds of the air; they do not sow or reap or store away in barns, and yet your heavenly Father feeds them. Are you not much more valuable than they? *Matthew 6:25–26* NIV

**PRAYER:** Glory in His holy name; Let the heart of those who seek the LORD be glad. ⁴Seek the LORD and His strength; Seek His face continually. *Psalms 105:3–4* NAS95

**CHALLENGE:** The next day Jesus decided to go to Galilee. He found Philip and said to him, "Follow me." *John 1:43* ESV

## ∞ NOVEMBER 2 ∞

*Memory Verse 22*

**PROMISE:** I tell you the solemn truth, a time is coming—and is now here—when the dead will hear the voice of the Son of God, and those who hear will live. ²⁶For just as the Father has life in himself, thus he has granted the Son to have life in himself, ²⁷and he has granted the Son authority to execute judgment, because he is the Son of Man. *John 5:25–27* NET

**PRAYER:** Praise the LORD! Praise the name of the LORD; Praise Him, O servants of the LORD, ²You who stand in the house of the

LORD, In the courts of the house of our God! ³Praise the LORD, for the LORD is good; Sing praises to His name, for it is lovely. *Psalms 135:1–3* NAS95

**CHALLENGE:** We love because he first loved us. ²⁰If anyone says, "I love God," yet hates his brother, he is a liar. For anyone who does not love his brother, whom he has seen, cannot love God, whom he has not seen. *1 John 4:19–20* NIV

## ✂ NOVEMBER 3 ✂

*Memory Verse 22*

**PROMISE:** GOD, the Lord, is my strength; he makes my feet like the deer's; he makes me tread on my high places. To the choirmaster: with stringed instruments. *Habakkuk 3:19* ESV

**PRAYER:** ¹⁴But I trust in you, O LORD; I say, "You are my God." ¹⁵My times are in your hands; deliver me from my enemies and from those who pursue me. *Psalms 31:13–15* NIV

**CHALLENGE:** God blessed them and said to them, "Be fruitful and increase in number; fill the earth and subdue it. Rule over the fish of the sea and the birds of the air and over every living creature that moves on the ground." ²⁹Then God said, "I give you every seed-bearing plant on the face of the whole earth and every tree that has fruit with seed in it. They will be yours for food. ³⁰And to all the beasts of the earth and all the birds of the air and all the creatures that move on the ground—everything that has the breath of life in it—I give every green plant for food." And it was so. *Genesis 1:28–30* NIV

## ✂ NOVEMBER 4 ✂

*Memory Verse 22*

**PROMISE:** The LORD is King forever and ever; Nations have perished from His land. *Psalms 10:16* NAS95

**PRAYER:** Then Jesus spoke to them again: "I am the light of the world. Anyone who follows Me will never walk in the darkness but will have the light of life." *John 8:12* HCSB

**CHALLENGE:** And all the tithe of the land, whether of the seed of the land or of the fruit of the tree, is the LORD'S. It is holy to the LORD. ³¹If a man wants at all to redeem any of his tithes, he shall add one-fifth to it. ³²And concerning the tithe of the herd or the flock, of whatever passes under the rod, the tenth one shall be holy to the LORD. ³³He shall not inquire whether it is good or bad, nor shall he exchange it; and if he exchanges it at all, then both it and the one exchanged for it shall be holy; it shall not be redeemed. *Leviticus 27:30–33* NKJV

## ℘ NOVEMBER 5 ℀

*Memory Verse 22*

**PROMISE:** For the wages of sin is death, but the free gift of God is eternal life in Christ Jesus our Lord. *Romans 6:23* ESV

**PRAYER:** I desperately long for your deliverance. I find hope in your word. *Psalms 119:81* NET

**CHALLENGE:** But above all, my brothers, do not swear, either by heaven or by earth or by any other oath, but let your "yes" be yes and your "no" be no, so that you may not fall under condemnation. *James 5:12* ESV

## ℘ NOVEMBER 6 ℀

*Memory Verse 22*

**PROMISE:** Blow the trumpet in Zion, And sound an alarm in My holy mountain! Let all the inhabitants of the land tremble; For the day of the LORD is coming, For it is at hand: *Joel 2:1* NKJV

**PRAYER:** Don't be terrified or afraid. Didn't I make this known to you long ago? You are my witnesses. Is there any God except me? There is no ‹other› rock; I know of none. *Isaiah 44:8* GWORD

**CHALLENGE:** And He said to him, "'YOU SHALL LOVE THE LORD YOUR GOD WITH ALL YOUR HEART, AND WITH ALL YOUR SOUL, AND WITH ALL YOUR MIND.' ³⁸ "This is the great and foremost commandment. ³⁹ "The second is like it, 'YOU SHALL LOVE YOUR NEIGHBOR AS YOURSELF.' ⁴⁰ "On these two commandments depend the whole Law and the Prophets." *Matthew 22:37–40* NAS95

# ❧ NOVEMBER 7 ☙

*Memory Verse 23*

**PROMISE:** But you will receive power when the Holy Spirit comes on you; and you will be my witnesses in Jerusalem, and in all Judea and Samaria, and to the ends of the earth." *Acts 1:8* NIV

**PRAYER:** I pray that the perception of your mind may be enlightened so you may know what is the hope of His calling, what are the glorious riches of His inheritance among the saints, ¹⁹and what is the immeasurable greatness of His power to us who believe, according to the working of His vast strength. *Ephesians 1:18–19* HCSB

**CHALLENGE:** A new commandment I give to you, that you love one another: just as I have loved you, you also are to love one another. ³⁵By this all people will know that you are my disciples, if you have love for one another." *John 13:34–35* ESV

# ❧ NOVEMBER 8 ☙

*Memory Verse 23*

**PROMISE:** Now it is God who makes both us and you stand firm in Christ. He anointed us, ²²set his seal of ownership on us, and put his Spirit in our hearts as a deposit, guaranteeing what is to come. *2 Corinthians 1:21–22* NIV

**PRAYER:** Blessed be the LORD, the God of Israel, From everlasting even to everlasting. And let all the people say, "Amen." Praise the LORD! *Psalms 106:48* NAS95

**CHALLENGE:** But you, man of God, must avoid these things. Pursue what God approves of: a godly life, faith, love, endurance, and gentleness. ¹²Fight the good fight for the Christian faith. Take hold of everlasting life to which you were called and about which you made a good testimony in front of many witnesses. *1 Timothy 6:11–12* GWORD

## ᢒ NOVEMBER 9 ᢒ

*Memory Verse 23*

**PROMISE:** When the whirlwind passes by, the wicked is no more, But the righteous has an everlasting foundation. *Proverbs 10:25* NKJV

**PRAYER:** LORD, be gracious to us! We wait for You. Be our strength every morning and our salvation in time of trouble. *Isaiah 33:2* HCSB

**CHALLENGE:** Then the King will say to those on His right, 'Come, you who are blessed of My Father, inherit the kingdom prepared for you from the foundation of the world. ³⁵'For I was hungry, and you gave Me something to eat; I was thirsty, and you gave Me something to drink; I was a stranger, and you invited Me in; ³⁶naked, and you clothed Me; I was sick, and you visited Me; I was in prison, and you came to Me.' *Matthew 25:34–36* NAS95

## ᢒ NOVEMBER 10 ᢒ

*Memory Verse 23*

**PROMISE:** The LORD will be awesome to them, For He will reduce to nothing all the gods of the earth; People shall worship Him, Each one from his place, Indeed all the shores of the nations. *Zephaniah 2:11* NKJV

**PRAYER:** And the LORD has rewarded me according to my righteousness, according to my cleanness in his sight. *2 Samuel 22:25* ESV

**CHALLENGE:** "Honor your father and your mother, so that you may live long in the land the LORD your God is giving you. *Exodus 20:12–13* NIV

## ❧ NOVEMBER 11 ☙

*Memory Verse 23*

**PROMISE:** and human hands can't serve his needs—for he has no needs. He himself gives life and breath to everything, and he satisfies every need. ²⁶From one man he created all the nations throughout the whole earth. He decided beforehand when they should rise and fall, and he determined their boundaries. *Acts 17:25–26* NLT

**PRAYER:** My soul yearns for you in the night; my spirit within me earnestly seeks you. *Isaiah 26:9* ESV

**CHALLENGE:** It is good to give thanks to the LORD, And to sing praises to Your name, O Most High; ²To declare Your lovingkindness in the morning, And Your faithfulness every night, ³On an instrument of ten strings, On the lute, And on the harp, With harmonious sound. *Psalms 92:1–3* NKJV

## ❧ NOVEMBER 12 ☙

*Memory Verse 23*

**PROMISE:** As many as I love, I rebuke and discipline. So be committed and repent. ²⁰Listen! I stand at the door and knock. If anyone hears My voice and opens the door, I will come in to him and have dinner with him, and he with Me. *Revelation 3:19–20* HCSB

**PRAYER:** Behold, bless the LORD, all servants of the LORD, Who serve by night in the house of the LORD! ²Lift up your hands to the sanctuary And bless the LORD. ³May the LORD bless you from Zion, He who made heaven and earth. *Psalms 134:1–3* NAS95

**CHALLENGE:** Listen with respect to the father who raised you, and when your mother grows old, don't neglect her. *Proverbs 23:22* MESSAGE

## ℘ NOVEMBER 13 ℘

*Memory Verse 23*

**PROMISE:** This is love for God: to obey his commands. And his commands are not burdensome, ⁴for everyone born of God overcomes the world. This is the victory that has overcome the world, even our faith. ⁵Who is it that overcomes the world? Only he who believes that Jesus is the Son of God. *1 John 5:3–5* NIV

**PRAYER:** Do not be anxious about anything. Instead, in every situation, through prayer and petition with thanksgiving, tell your requests to God. ⁷And the peace of God that surpasses all understanding will guard your hearts and minds in Christ Jesus. *Philippians 4:6–7* NET

**CHALLENGE:** Trust in the LORD with all your heart And do not lean on your own understanding. *Proverbs 3:5* NAS95

## ℘ NOVEMBER 14 ℘

*Memory Verse 23*

**PROMISE:** This is the book of the generations of Adam. In the day when God created man, He made him in the likeness of God. ²He created them male and female, and He blessed them and named them Man in the day when they were created. *Genesis 5:1–2* NAS95

**PRAYER:** O give thanks unto the LORD, for he is good: for his mercy endureth for ever. *Psalms 107:1* KJV

**CHALLENGE:** Charm is deceptive, and beauty is fleeting; but a woman who fears the LORD is to be praised. ³¹Give her the reward she has earned, and let her works bring her praise at the city gate. *Proverbs 31:30–31* NIV

## ಲ NOVEMBER **15** ಣ

*Memory Verse 23*

**PROMISE:** For this God is our God for ever and ever: he will be our guide even unto death. *Psalms 48:14* KJV

**PRAYER:** Jabez cried out to the God of Israel, "Oh, that you would bless me and enlarge my territory! Let your hand be with me, and keep me from harm so that I will be free from pain." And God granted his request. *1 Chronicles 4:10* NIV

**CHALLENGE:** Learn to do good. Seek justice. Help the oppressed. Defend the cause of orphans. Fight for the rights of widows. *Isaiah 1:17* NLT

## ಲ NOVEMBER **16** ಣ

*Memory Verse 23*

**PROMISE:** "Listen! We are going up to Jerusalem. The Son of Man will be handed over to the chief priests and the scribes, and they will condemn Him to death. Then they will hand Him over to the Gentiles, ³⁴and they will mock Him, spit on Him, flog Him, and kill Him, and He will rise after three days." *Mark 10:33–34* HCSB

**PRAYER:** Examine me, and probe my thoughts! Test me, and know my concerns! ²⁴See if there is any idolatrous tendency in me, and lead me in the reliable ancient path! *Psalms 139:23–24* NET

**CHALLENGE:** So commit yourselves wholeheartedly to these words of mine. Tie them to your hands and wear them on your forehead as reminders. ¹⁹Teach them to your children. Talk about them when you are at home and when you are on the road, when you are going to bed and when you are getting up. ²⁰Write them on the doorposts of your house and on your gates, *Deuteronomy 11:18–20* NLT

## ❧ NOVEMBER 17 ❧

*Memory Verse 23*

**PROMISE:** Wise words bring many benefits, and hard work brings rewards. *Proverbs 12:14* NLT

**PRAYER:** Shower, O heavens, from above, and let the clouds rain down righteousness; let the earth open, that salvation and righteousness may bear fruit; let the earth cause them both to sprout; I the LORD have created it. *Isaiah 45:8* ESV

**CHALLENGE:** "You shall not murder. ¹⁴"You shall not commit adultery. ¹⁵"You shall not steal. ¹⁶"You shall not give false testimony against your neighbor. *Exodus 20:13–16* NIV

## ❧ NOVEMBER 18 ❧

*Memory Verse 23*

**PROMISE:** But I told you that you have seen me and still do not believe. ³⁷Everyone whom the Father gives me will come to me, and the one who comes to me I will never send away. *John 6:36–37* NET

**PRAYER:** Yet You are our Father, even though Abraham does not know us and Israel doesn't recognize us. You, Yahweh, are our Father; from ancient times, Your name is our Redeemer. *Isaiah 63:16* HCSB

**CHALLENGE:** My son, do not forget my law, But let your heart keep my commands; *Proverbs 3:1* NKJV

## ❧ NOVEMBER 19 ❧

*Memory Verse 23*

**PROMISE:** But Samuel replied, "What is more pleasing to the LORD: your burnt offerings and sacrifices or your obedience to his voice? Listen! Obedience is better than sacrifice, and submission is better than offering the fat of rams. ²³Rebellion is as sinful as witch-craft, and stubbornness as bad as worshiping idols. So because you have rejected the command of the LORD, he has rejected you as king." *1 Samuel 15:22–23* NLT

**PRAYER:** Our Lord and God, You are worthy to receive glory and honor and power, because You have created all things, and because of Your will they exist and were created. *Revelation 4:11* HCSB

**CHALLENGE:** May I be fully committed to your statutes, so that I might not be ashamed. *Psalms 119:80* NET

## ✂ NOVEMBER 20 ✂

*Memory Verse 23*

**PROMISE:** "But when the Son of Man comes in His glory, and all the angels with Him, then He will sit on His glorious throne. ³²"All the nations will be gathered before Him; and He will separate them from one another, as the shepherd separates the sheep from the goats; ³³and He will put the sheep on His right, and the goats on the left. *Matthew 25:31–33* NAS95

**PRAYER:** I will say of the LORD, "He is my refuge and my fortress; My God, in Him I will trust." *Psalms 91:2* NKJV

**CHALLENGE:** As you enter the house of God, keep your ears open and your mouth shut. It is evil to make mindless offerings to God. ²Don't make rash promises, and don't be hasty in bringing matters before God. After all, God is in heaven, and you are here on earth. So let your words be few. *Ecclesiastes 5:1–2* NLT

## ✂ NOVEMBER 21 ✂

*Memory Verse 24*

**PROMISE:** He who has My commandments and keeps them, it is he who loves Me. And he who loves Me will be loved by My Father, and I will love him and manifest Myself to him." *John 14:21* NKJV

**PRAYER:** Some people pour out their silver and gold and hire a craftsman to make a god from it. Then they bow down and worship it! ⁷They carry it around on their shoulders, and when they set it down, it stays there. It can't even move! And when someone prays to it, there is no answer. It can't rescue anyone from trouble. *Isaiah 46:6–7* NLT

**CHALLENGE:** Do not set foot on the path of the wicked or walk in the way of evil men. ¹⁵Avoid it, do not travel on it; turn from it and go on your way. *Proverbs 4:14–15* NIV

## ∾ NOVEMBER 22 ∾

*Memory Verse 24*

**PROMISE:** Therefore say to them, "Thus says the LORD of hosts: 'Return to Me,'" says the LORD of hosts, "and I will return to you," says the LORD of hosts. *Zechariah 1:3* NKJV

**PRAYER:** In God, whose word I praise, in the LORD, whose word I praise—¹¹in God I trust; I will not be afraid. What can man do to me? *Psalms 56:10–11* NIV

**CHALLENGE:** Remind the believers to submit to the government and its officers. They should be obedient, always ready to do what is good. ²They must not slander anyone and must avoid quarreling. Instead, they should be gentle and show true humility to everyone. *Titus 3:1–2* NLT

## ∾ NOVEMBER 23 ∾

*Memory Verse 24*

**PROMISE:** A good person's mouth is a clear fountain of wisdom; a foul mouth is a stagnant swamp. *Proverbs 10:31* MESSAGE

**PRAYER:** ³I will praise thee, O LORD, among the people: and I will sing praises unto thee among the nations. ⁴For thy mercy is great above the heavens: and thy truth reacheth unto the clouds. *Psalms 108:2–4* KJV

**CHALLENGE:** Jesus called them over and said to them, "You know that those who are regarded as rulers of the Gentiles dominate them, and their men of high positions exercise power over them. ⁴³But it must not be like that among you. On the contrary, whoever wants to become great among you must be your servant, ⁴⁴and whoever wants to be first among you must be a slave to all. ⁴⁵For even the Son of Man did not come to be served, but to serve, and to give His life—a ransom for many." *Mark 10:42–45* HCSB

## ℘ NOVEMBER 24 ℘

### *Memory Verse 24*

**PROMISE:** Do not let this Book of the Law depart from your mouth; meditate on it day and night, so that you may be careful to do everything written in it. Then you will be prosperous and successful. *Joshua 1:8* NIV

**PRAYER:** And, "YOU, LORD, IN THE BEGINNING LAID THE FOUNDATION OF THE EARTH, AND THE HEAVENS ARE THE WORKS OF YOUR HANDS; ¹¹THEY WILL PERISH, BUT YOU REMAIN; AND THEY ALL WILL BECOME OLD LIKE A GARMENT, ¹²AND LIKE A MANTLE YOU WILL ROLL THEM UP; LIKE A GARMENT THEY WILL ALSO BE CHANGED. BUT YOU ARE THE SAME, AND YOUR YEARS WILL NOT COME TO AN END." *Hebrews 1:10–12* NAS95

**CHALLENGE:** O LORD, God of my salvation; I cry out day and night before you. *Psalms 88:1* ESV

## ℘ NOVEMBER 25 ℘

### *Memory Verse 24*

**PROMISE:** The adversaries of the LORD shall be broken in pieces; From heaven He will thunder against them. The LORD will judge the ends of the earth. "He will give strength to His king, And exalt the horn of His anointed." *1 Samuel 2:10* NKJV

**PRAYER:** Let your face shine on your servant; save me in your unfailing love. *Psalms 31:16* NIV

**CHALLENGE:** Now I urge you, brothers, in the name of our Lord Jesus Christ, that all of you agree in what you say, that there be no divisions among you, and that you be united with the same understanding and the same conviction. *1 Corinthians 1:10* HCSB

## ೞ NOVEMBER 26 ೞ

### *Memory Verse 24*

**PROMISE:** Our days on earth are like grass; like wildflowers, we bloom and die. ¹⁶The wind blows, and we are gone—as though we had never been here. ¹⁷But the love of the LORD remains forever with those who fear him. His salvation extends to the children's children ¹⁸of those who are faithful to his covenant, of those who obey his commandments! *Psalms 103:15–18* NLT

**PRAYER:** ³When you pray for things, you don't get them because you want them for the wrong reason—for your own pleasure. *James 4:2–3* GWORD

**CHALLENGE:** Rejoice with those who rejoice, and weep with those who weep. ¹⁶Be of the same mind toward one another. Do not set your mind on high things, but associate with the humble. Do not be wise in your own opinion. *Romans 12:15–16* NKJV

## ೞ NOVEMBER 27 ೞ

### *Memory Verse 24*

**PROMISE:** For the LORD is righteous, He loves righteousness; The upright will behold His face. *Psalms 11:7* NAS95

**PRAYER:** For behold, He who forms mountains, And creates the wind, Who declares to man what his thought is, And makes the morning darkness, Who treads the high places of the earth—The LORD God of hosts is His name. *Amos 4:13* NKJV

**CHALLENGE:** You are from below," He told them, "I am from above. You are of this world; I am not of this world. ²⁴Therefore I told you that you will die in your sins. For if you do not believe that I am He, you will die in your sins." *John 8:23–24* HCSB

## ✎ NOVEMBER 28 ✎

*Memory Verse 24*

**PROMISE:** Truly, truly, I say to you, whoever receives the one I send receives me, and whoever receives me receives the one who sent me." *John 13:20* ESV

**PRAYER:** I pray that the God of our Lord Jesus Christ, the glorious Father, would give you a spirit of wisdom and revelation in the knowledge of Him. *Ephesians 1:17* HCSB

**CHALLENGE:** I find delight in your statutes; I do not forget your instructions. *Psalms 119:16* NET

## ✎ NOVEMBER 29 ✎

*Memory Verse 24*

**PROMISE:** There is no difference, ²³for all have sinned and fall short of the glory of God, ²⁴and are justified freely by his grace through the redemption that came by Christ Jesus. ²⁵God presented him as a sacrifice of atonement, through faith in his blood. He did this to demonstrate his justice, because in his forbearance he had left the sins committed beforehand unpunished—*Romans 3:22–25* NIV

**PRAYER:** I am Yahweh, and there is no other; there is no God but Me. I will strengthen you, though you do not know Me, ⁶so that all may know from the rising of the sun to its setting that there is no one but Me. I am Yahweh, and there is no other. *Isaiah 45:5–6* HCSB

**CHALLENGE:** Do not let your heart envy sinners, But live in the fear of the LORD always. ¹⁸Surely there is a future, And your hope will not be cut off. *Proverbs 23:17–18* NAS95

## ℰ NOVEMBER **30** ℭ

*Memory Verse 24*

**PROMISE:** For he has set a day for judging the world with justice by the man he has appointed, and he proved to everyone who this is by raising him from the dead." *Acts 17:31* NLT

**PRAYER:** For this is what the high and lofty One says—he who lives forever, whose name is holy: "I live in a high and holy place, but also with him who is contrite and lowly in spirit, to revive the spirit of the lowly and to revive the heart of the contrite. *Isaiah 57:15* NIV

**CHALLENGE:** Woe to you, scribes and Pharisees, hypocrites! For you clean the outside of the cup and of the dish, but inside they are full of robbery and self-indulgence. ²⁶ "You blind Pharisee, first clean the inside of the cup and of the dish, so that the outside of it may become clean also. *Matthew 23:25–26* NAS95

# December

## ☙ DECEMBER 1 ❧

*Memory Verse 24*

**PROMISE:** At the right time God will make this known. God is the blessed and only ruler. He is the King of kings and Lord of lords. [16]He is the only one who cannot die. He lives in light that no one can come near. No one has seen him, nor can they see him. Honor and power belong to him forever! Amen. *1 Timothy 6:15–16* GWORD

**PRAYER:** Therefore, confess your sins to one another and pray for one another, that you may be healed. The prayer of a righteous person has great power as it is working. *James 5:16* ESV

**CHALLENGE:** Do not be overcome by evil, but overcome evil with good. *Romans 12:21* NIV

## ☙ DECEMBER 2 ❧

*Memory Verse 24*

**PROMISE:** I'm setting up my covenant with you that never again will everything living be destroyed by floodwaters; no, never again will a flood destroy the Earth." [12]God continued, "This is the sign of the covenant I am making between me and you and everything living around you and everyone living after you. [13]I'm putting my rainbow in the clouds, a sign of the covenant between me and the Earth. *Genesis 9:11–13* MESSAGE

**PRAYER:** Your hands made me and formed me. Give me understanding so that I might learn your commands. *Psalms 119:73* NET

**CHALLENGE:** John answered, "The man with two tunics should share with him who has none, and the one who has food should do the same." *Luke 3:11* NIV

## ഌ DECEMBER 3 ര

*Memory Verse 24*

**PROMISE:** I will be your God throughout your lifetime—until your hair is white with age. I made you, and I will care for you. I will carry you along and save you. ⁵"To whom will you compare me? Who is my equal? *Isaiah 46:4–5* NLT

**PRAYER:** For you have delivered me from death and my feet from stumbling, that I may walk before God in the light of life. *Psalms 56:13* NIV

**CHALLENGE:** Stand therefore, having fastened on the belt of truth, and having put on the breastplate of righteousness, ¹⁵and, as shoes for your feet, having put on the readiness given by the gospel of peace. ¹⁶In all circumstances take up the shield of faith, with which you can extinguish all the flaming darts of the evil one; ¹⁷and take the helmet of salvation, and the sword of the Spirit, which is the word of God, ¹⁸praying at all times in the Spirit, with all prayer and supplication. To that end keep alert with all perseverance, making supplication for all the saints, *Ephesians 6:14–18* ESV

## ഌ DECEMBER 4 ര

*Memory Verse 24*

**PROMISE:** The lip of truth shall be established for ever: but a lying tongue is but for a moment. *Proverbs 12:19* KJV

**PRAYER:** With the merciful you show yourself merciful; with the blameless man you show yourself blameless; ²⁷with the purified you deal purely, and with the crooked you make yourself seem tortuous. *2 Samuel 22:26–27* ESV

**CHALLENGE:** Do not lack diligence; be fervent in spirit; serve the Lord. *Romans 12:11* HCSB

## ஐ DECEMBER 5 ଔ

*Memory Verse 25*

**PROMISE:** The nations will walk in its light, and the kings of the world will enter the city in all their glory. ²⁵Its gates will never be closed at the end of day because there is no night there. ²⁶And all the nations will bring their glory and honor into the city. ²⁷Nothing evil will be allowed to enter, nor anyone who practices shameful idolatry and dishonesty—but only those whose names are written in the Lamb's Book of Life. *Revelation 21:24–27* NLT

**PRAYER:** Help me, O LORD my God; Save me according to Your lovingkindness. ²⁷And let them know that this is Your hand; You, LORD, have done it. *Psalms 109:26–27* NAS95

**CHALLENGE:** Don't be afraid to correct your young ones; a spanking won't kill them. ¹⁴A good spanking, in fact, might save them from something worse than death. *Proverbs 23:13–14* MESSAGE

## ஐ DECEMBER 6 ଔ

*Memory Verse 25*

**PROMISE:** In all your ways acknowledge Him, And He will make your paths straight. *Proverbs 3:6* NAS95

**PRAYER:** When I consider your heavens, the work of your fingers, the moon and the stars, which you have set in place, ⁴what is man that you are mindful of him, the son of man that you care for him? ⁵You made him a little lower than the heavenly beings and crowned him with glory and honor. *Psalms 8:3–5* NIV

**CHALLENGE:** We intend to do what is right, not only in the sight of the Lord, but also in the sight of people. *2 Corinthians 8:21* GWORD

## ∽ DECEMBER 7 ∾

*Memory Verse 25*

**PROMISE:** But—"When God our Savior revealed his kindness and love, ⁵he saved us, not because of the righteous things we had done, but because of his mercy. He washed away our sins, giving us a new birth and new life through the Holy Spirit. *Titus 3:4–5* NLT

**PRAYER:** Satisfy us every morning with your mercy so that we may sing joyfully and rejoice all our days. *Psalms 90:14* GWORD

**CHALLENGE:** But Peter and John spoke right back, "Whether it's right in God's eyes to listen to you rather than to God, you decide. ²⁰As for us, there's no question—we can't keep quiet about what we've seen and heard." *Acts 4:19–20* MESSAGE

## ∽ DECEMBER 8 ∾

*Memory Verse 25*

**PROMISE:** "Therefore, this is the declaration of the LORD, the God of Israel: 'Although I said your family and your ancestral house would walk before Me forever, the LORD now says, "No longer!" I will honor those who honor Me, but those who despise Me will be disgraced. *1 Samuel 2:30* HCSB

**PRAYER:** I will go before you and make the rough places smooth; I will shatter the doors of bronze and cut through their iron bars. ³"I will give you the treasures of darkness And hidden wealth of secret places, So that you may know that it is I, The LORD, the God of Israel, who calls you by your name. *Isaiah 45:2–3* NAS95

**CHALLENGE:** Work hard and become a leader; be lazy and become a slave. *Proverbs 12:24* NLT

## ᏸ DECEMBER **9** ᏻ

*Memory Verse 25*

**PROMISE:** But I tell you that something greater than the temple is here! ⁷If you had known what this means: I desire mercy and not sacrifice, you would not have condemned the innocent. ⁸For the Son of Man is Lord of the Sabbath." *Matthew 12:6–8* HCSB

**PRAYER:** God is faithful, by whom ye were called unto the fellowship of his Son Jesus Christ our Lord. *1 Corinthians 1:9* KJV

**CHALLENGE:** Open your mouth for the mute, For the rights of all the unfortunate. ⁹Open your mouth, judge righteously, And defend the rights of the afflicted and needy. *Proverbs 31:8–9* NAS95

## ᏸ DECEMBER **10** ᏻ

*Memory Verse 25*

**PROMISE:** It came to pass in those days that Jesus came from Nazareth of Galilee, and was baptized by John in the Jordan. ¹⁰And immediately, coming up from the water, He saw the heavens parting and the Spirit descending upon Him like a dove. ¹¹Then a voice came from heaven, "You are My beloved Son, in whom I am well pleased." *Mark 1:9–11* NKJV

**PRAYER:** Ascribe to the LORD, O clans of the peoples, ascribe to the LORD glory and strength! ²⁹Ascribe to the LORD the glory due his name; bring an offering and come before him! *1 Chronicles 16:28–29* ESV

**CHALLENGE:** One night the Lord spoke to Paul in a vision and told him, "Don't be afraid! Speak out! Don't be silent! ¹⁰For I am with you, and no one will attack and harm you, for many people in this city belong to me." *Acts 18:9–10* NLT

## ഇ DECEMBER 11 ⊗

*Memory Verse 25*

**PROMISE:** As He was going out of the temple complex, one of His disciples said to Him, "Teacher, look! What massive stones! What impressive buildings!" ²Jesus said to him, "Do you see these great buildings? Not one stone will be left here on another that will not be thrown down!" *Mark 13:1–2* HCSB

**PRAYER:** Be kind to your servant! Then I will live and keep your instructions. ¹⁸Open my eyes so I can truly see the marvelous things in your law! *Psalms 119:17–18* NET

**CHALLENGE:** You therefore must endure hardship as a good soldier of Jesus Christ. *2 Timothy 2:3* NKJV

## ഇ DECEMBER 12 ⊗

*Memory Verse 25*

**PROMISE:** In the beginning was the Word, and the Word was with God, and the Word was God. ²He was in the beginning with God. ³All things were made through him, and without him was not any thing made that was made. ⁴In him was life, and the life was the light of men. ⁵The light shines in the darkness, and the darkness has not overcome it. *John 1:1–5* ESV

**PRAYER:** but to the Son: Your throne, God, is forever and ever, and the scepter of Your kingdom is a scepter of justice. ⁹You have loved righteousness and hated lawlessness; this is why God, Your God, has anointed You with the oil of joy rather than Your companions. *Hebrews 1:8–9* HCSB

**CHALLENGE:** Oh come, let us sing to the LORD; let us make a joyful noise to the rock of our salvation! ²Let us come into his presence with thanksgiving; let us make a joyful noise to him with songs of praise! *Psalms 95:1–2* ESV

## ເ∾ DECEMBER **13** ୦ଛ

*Memory Verse 25*

**PROMISE:** My brothers, if anyone among you wanders from the truth and someone brings him back, ²⁰let him know that whoever brings back a sinner from his wandering will save his soul from death and will cover a multitude of sins. *James 5:19–20* ESV

**PRAYER:** praise him with tambourine and dancing, praise him with the strings and flute, ⁵praise him with the clash of cymbals, praise him with resounding cymbals. ⁶Let everything that has breath praise the LORD. Praise the LORD. *Psalms 150:4–6* NIV

**CHALLENGE:** If we are thrown into the blazing furnace, the God whom we serve is able to save us. He will rescue us from your power, Your Majesty. ¹⁸But even if he doesn't, we want to make it clear to you, Your Majesty, that we will never serve your gods or worship the gold statue you have set up." *Daniel 3:17–18* NLT

## ເ∾ DECEMBER **14** ୦ଛ

*Memory Verse 25*

**PROMISE:** "This is my promise to them," says the Lord. "My Spirit, who is on you, and my words that I put in your mouth will not leave you. They will be with your children and your grandchildren permanently," says the Lord. *Isaiah 59:21* GWORD

**PRAYER:** But I have trusted in Your lovingkindness; My heart shall rejoice in Your salvation. ⁶I will sing to the LORD, Because He has dealt bountifully with me. *Psalms 13:5–6* NAS95

**CHALLENGE:** Whoever seeks to preserve his life will lose it, but whoever loses his life will keep it. *Luke 17:33–34* ESV

## ಏಂ DECEMBER 15 ಞ

*Memory Verse 25*

**PROMISE:** For I am sure that neither death nor life, nor angels nor rulers, nor things present nor things to come, nor powers, [39]nor height nor depth, nor anything else in all creation, will be able to separate us from the love of God in Christ Jesus our Lord. *Romans 8:38–39* ESV

**PRAYER:** Now may the God of peace himself make you completely holy and may your spirit and soul and body be kept entirely blameless at the coming of our Lord Jesus Christ. *1 Thessalonians 5:23* NET

**CHALLENGE:** Live a more disciplined life, and listen carefully to words of knowledge. *Proverbs 23:12* GWORD

## ಏಂ DECEMBER 16 ಞ

*Memory Verse 25*

**PROMISE:** In Him we have redemption through His blood, the forgiveness of our trespasses, according to the riches of His grace [8]which He lavished on us. In all wisdom and insight *Ephesians 1:7–8* NAS95

**PRAYER:** O Lord, you have been our refuge throughout every generation. [2]Before the mountains were born, before you gave birth to the earth and the world, you were God. You are God from everlasting to everlasting. *Psalms 90:1–2* GWORD

**CHALLENGE:** "Why do you look at the speck in your brother's eye, but don't notice the log in your own eye? *Luke 6:41* HCSB

## ಏಂ DECEMBER 17 ಞ

*Memory Verse 25*

**PROMISE:** "Heaven and earth will pass away, but My words will not pass away. [36]"But of that day and hour no one knows, not even the angels of heaven, nor the Son, but the Father alone. *Matthew 24:35–36* NAS95

**PRAYER:** "Two things I ask of you, O LORD; do not refuse me before I die: ⁸Keep falsehood and lies far from me; give me neither poverty nor riches, but give me only my daily bread. ⁹Otherwise, I may have too much and disown you and say, 'Who is the LORD?' Or I may become poor and steal, and so dishonor the name of my God. *Proverbs 30:7–9* NIV

**CHALLENGE:** The Lord is waiting to be kind to you. He rises to have compassion on you. The Lord is a God of justice. Blessed are all those who wait for him. *Isaiah 30:18* GWORD

## ℘ DECEMBER 18 ℘

### *Memory Verse 25*

**PROMISE:** Who of you by worrying can add a single hour to his life? ²⁸"And why do you worry about clothes? See how the lilies of the field grow. They do not labor or spin. ²⁹Yet I tell you that not even Solomon in all his splendor was dressed like one of these. ³⁰If that is how God clothes the grass of the field, which is here today and tomorrow is thrown into the fire, will he not much more clothe you, O you of little faith? *Matthew 6:27–30* NIV

**PRAYER:** With my mouth I will give thanks abundantly to the LORD; And in the midst of many I will praise Him. ³¹For He stands at the right hand of the needy, To save him from those who judge his soul. *Psalms 109:30–31* NAS95

**CHALLENGE:** Love each other. This is what I'm commanding you to do. *John 15:17* GWORD

## ᏻᏜ DECEMBER 19 ᏒᎡ

*Memory Verse 26*

**PROMISE:** For unto us a Child is born, Unto us a Son is given; And the government will be upon His shoulder. And His name will be called Wonderful, Counselor, Mighty God, Everlasting Father, Prince of Peace. *Isaiah 9:6* NKJV

**PRAYER:** Let the heavens praise your wonders, O LORD, your faithfulness in the assembly of the holy ones! [6]For who in the skies can be compared to the LORD? Who among the heavenly beings is like the LORD, [7]a God greatly to be feared in the council of the holy ones, and awesome above all who are around him? *Psalms 89:5–7* ESV

**CHALLENGE:** Tell those who have the riches of this world not to be arrogant and not to place their confidence in anything as uncertain as riches. Instead, they should place their confidence in God who richly provides us with everything to enjoy. [18]Tell them to do good, to do a lot of good things, to be generous, and to share. [19]By doing this they store up a treasure for themselves which is a good foundation for the future. In this way they take hold of what life really is. *1 Timothy 6:17–19* GWORD

## ᏻᏜ DECEMBER 20 ᏒᎡ

*Memory Verse 26*

**PROMISE:** One man gives freely, yet gains even more; another withholds unduly, but comes to poverty. [25]A generous man will prosper; he who refreshes others will himself be refreshed. *Proverbs 11:24–25* NIV

**PRAYER:** And the Word became flesh and dwelt among us, and we have seen his glory, glory as of the only Son from the Father, full of grace and truth. *John 1:14* ESV

**CHALLENGE:** Bless those who persecute you; bless and do not curse. *Romans 12:14* NKJV

## ❧ DECEMBER 21 ☙

*Memory Verse 26*

**PROMISE:** Therefore, if anyone is in Christ, he is a new creation. The old has passed away; behold, the new has come. *2 Corinthians 5:17* ESV

**PRAYER:** I tell you the truth, you can say to this mountain, 'May you be lifted up and thrown into the sea,' and it will happen. But you must really believe it will happen and have no doubt in your heart. <sup>24</sup>I tell you, you can pray for anything, and if you believe that you've received it, it will be yours. *Mark 11:23–24* NLT

**CHALLENGE:** Therefore, God's chosen ones, holy and loved, put on heartfelt compassion, kindness, humility, gentleness, and patience, <sup>13</sup>accepting one another and forgiving one another if anyone has a complaint against another. Just as the Lord has forgiven you, so you must also forgive. <sup>14</sup>Above all, put on love—the perfect bond of unity. *Colossians 3:12–14* HCSB

## ❧ DECEMBER 22 ☙

*Memory Verse 26*

**PROMISE:** GOD has set his throne in heaven; he rules over us all. He's the King! *Psalms 103:19* MESSAGE

**PRAYER:** When they saw the star, they were overjoyed beyond measure. <sup>11</sup>Entering the house, they saw the child with Mary His mother, and falling to their knees, they worshiped Him. Then they opened their treasures and presented Him with gifts: gold, frankincense, and myrrh. *Matthew 2:10–12* HCSB

**CHALLENGE:** Do not wear yourself out getting rich. Be smart enough to stop. *Proverbs 23:4* GWORD

## ♠ DECEMBER 23 ♠

*Memory Verse 26*

**PROMISE:** See that what you have heard from the beginning remains in you. If it does, you also will remain in the Son and in the Father. ²⁵And this is what he promised us—even eternal life. *1 John 2:24–25* NIV

**PRAYER:** Great are the works of the LORD; They are studied by all who delight in them. ³Splendid and majestic is His work, And His righteousness endures forever. *Psalms 111:2–3* NAS95

**CHALLENGE:** You are from below," He told them, "I am from above. You are of this world; I am not of this world. ²⁴Therefore I told you that you will die in your sins. For if you do not believe that I am He, you will die in your sins." *John 8:23–24* HCSB

## ♠ DECEMBER 24 ♠

*Memory Verse 26*

**PROMISE:** Whoever believes and is baptized will be saved, but whoever does not believe will be condemned. *Mark 16:16* ESV

**PRAYER:** Cry out, "Save us, O God our Savior; gather us and deliver us from the nations, that we may give thanks to your holy name, that we may glory in your praise." ³⁶Praise be to the LORD, the God of Israel, from everlasting to everlasting. Then all the people said "Amen" and "Praise the LORD." *1 Chronicles 16:35–36* NIV

**CHALLENGE:** But be alert at all times, praying that you may have strength to escape all these things that are going to take place and to stand before the Son of Man." *Luke 21:36* HCSB

## ❧ DECEMBER 25 ☙

*Memory Verse 26*

**PROMISE:** See, the virgin will become pregnant and give birth to a son, and they will name Him Immanuel, which is translated "God is with us." *Matthew 1:23* HCSB

**PRAYER:** The Lord is our judge. The Lord is our lawgiver. The Lord is our king. The Lord is our savior. *Isaiah 33:22* GWORD

**CHALLENGE:** But my life is worth nothing to me unless I use it for finishing the work assigned me by the Lord Jesus—the work of telling others the Good News about the wonderful grace of God. *Acts 20:24* NLT

## ❧ DECEMBER 26 ☙

*Memory Verse 26*

**PROMISE:** A man of many companions may come to ruin, but there is a friend who sticks closer than a brother. *Proverbs 18:24* ESV

**PRAYER:** So the stone was moved away from the entrance of the tomb. Jesus looked up and said, "Father, I thank you for hearing me. ⁴²I've known that you always hear me. However, I've said this so that the crowd standing around me will believe that you sent me." ⁴³After Jesus had said this, he shouted as loudly as he could, "Lazarus, come out!" ⁴⁴The dead man came out. Strips of cloth were wound around his feet and hands, and his face was wrapped with a handkerchief. Jesus told them, "Free Lazarus, and let him go." *John 11:41–44* GWORD

**CHALLENGE:** So he answered, "Do not fear, for those who are with us are more than those who are with them." *2 Kings 6:16* NAS95

## ☙ DECEMBER 27 ❧

*Memory Verse 26*

**PROMISE:** The LORD said to Abram: Go out from your land, your relatives, and your father's house to the land that I will show you. ²I will make you into a great nation, I will bless you, I will make your name great, and you will be a blessing. ³I will bless those who bless you, I will curse those who treat you with contempt, and all the peoples on earth will be blessed through you. *Genesis 12:1–3* HCSB

**PRAYER:** And a voice came out of the throne, saying, Praise our God, all ye his servants, and ye that fear him, both small and great. *Revelation 19:5* KJV

**CHALLENGE:** Behold, the LORD'S hand is not so short That it cannot save; Nor is His ear so dull That it cannot hear. ²But your iniquities have made a separation between you and your God, And your sins have hidden His face from you so that He does not hear. *Isaiah 59:1–2* NAS95

## ☙ DECEMBER 28 ❧

*Memory Verse 26*

**PROMISE:** Seldom set foot in your neighbor's house—too much of you, and he will hate you. *Proverbs 25:17* NIV

**PRAYER:** I thank my God always concerning you for the grace of God which was given you in Christ Jesus, ⁵that in everything you were enriched in Him, in all speech and all knowledge, ⁶even as the testimony concerning Christ was confirmed in you, ⁷so that you are not lacking in any gift, awaiting eagerly the revelation of our Lord Jesus Christ, ⁸who will also confirm you to the end, blameless in the day of our Lord Jesus Christ. *1 Corinthians 1:4–8* NAS95

**CHALLENGE:** Therefore be on the alert, for you do not know which day your Lord is coming. *Matthew 24:42* NAS95

## ᔓ DECEMBER **29** ᔕ

*Memory Verse 26*

**PROMISE:** He who walks blamelessly will be delivered, But he who is crooked will fall all at once. *Proverbs 28:18* NAS95

**PRAYER:** Praise the God and Father of our Lord Jesus Christ, who has blessed us in Christ with every spiritual blessing in the heavens. ⁴For He chose us in Him, before the foundation of the world, to be holy and blameless in His sight. *Ephesians 1:3–4* HCSB

**CHALLENGE:** The Lord has become my stronghold. My God has become my rock of refuge. *Psalms 94:22* GWORD

## ᔓ DECEMBER **30** ᔕ

*Memory Verse 26*

**PROMISE:** He hath made his wonderful works to be remembered: the LORD is gracious and full of compassion. *Psalms 111:4* KJV

**PRAYER:** The grace of our Lord Jesus Christ be with you all. Amen. *Revelation 22:21* NKJV

**CHALLENGE:** "Be careful that you don't forget the LORD your God by failing to keep His command—the ordinances and statutes—I am giving you today. ¹²When you eat and are full, and build beautiful houses to live in, ¹³and your herds and flocks grow large, and your silver and gold multiply, and everything else you have increases, ¹⁴be careful that your heart doesn't become proud and you forget the LORD your God who brought you out of the land of Egypt, out of the place of slavery. *Deuteronomy 8:11–14* HCSB

## ℰℐ DECEMBER 31 ℭℛ

*Memory Verse 26*

**PROMISE:** The Son is the radiance of God's glory and the exact representation of his being, sustaining all things by his powerful word. After he had provided purification for sins, he sat down at the right hand of the Majesty in heaven. ⁴So he became as much superior to the angels as the name he has inherited is superior to theirs. *Hebrews 1:3–4* NIV

**PRAYER:** You are good to your servant, O LORD, just as you promised. ⁶⁶Teach me proper discernment and understanding! For I consider your commands to be reliable. *Psalms 119:65–66* NET

**CHALLENGE:** If anyone among you thinks he is religious, and does not bridle his tongue but deceives his own heart, this one's religion is useless. ²⁷Pure and undefiled religion before God and the Father is this: to visit orphans and widows in their trouble, and to keep oneself unspotted from the world. *James 1:26–27* NKJV

# Appendix

## ☙ MEMORY VERSES ❧

| Level One | |
|---|---|
| 1. Philippians 2:14 | 14. Jeremiah 17:7 |
| 2. Psalms 23:1 | 15. Psalm 147:5 |
| 3. 1 Thessalonians 5:16-17 | 16. 1 Peter 5:7 |
| 4. 1 Corinthians 16:14 | 17. Philippians 4:13 |
| 5. John 15:17 | 18. Ephesians 4:2 |
| 6. Ephesians 6:1 | 19. 2 Corinthians 5:17 |
| 7. Philippians 4:4 | 20. Psalm 37:4 |
| 8. 1 John 5:3 | 21. Matthew 6:14 |
| 9. Psalm 145:9 | 22. John 13:34 |
| 10. John 10:30 | 23. 1 Peter 2:17 |
| 11. Exodus 20:12 | 24. Ephesians 4:32 |
| 12. Proverbs 17:17 | 25. Matthew 6:33 |
| 13. James 5:13 | 26. Psalm 62:1 |

| Level Two | | |
|---|---|---|
| 1. | 2 Timothy 2:16 | 14. Philippians 3:13-14 |
| 2. | John 14:6 | 15. James 2:18 |
| 3. | Proverbs 3:5-6 | 16. Psalms 18:1-2 |
| 4. | Matthew 11: 28-30 | 17. Lamentations 3:25–26 |
| 5. | Romans 5:6–8 | 18. Colossians 3:2 |
| 6. | Acts 20:24 | 19. Daniel 4:3 |
| 7. | 1 Corinthians 12:27 | 20. Romans 6:23 |
| 8. | Ephesians 4:29 | 21. Job 12:10 |
| 9. | Hebrews 11:1 | 22. 2 Timothy 4:2 |
| 10. | John 8:12 | 23. 1 Samuel 2:2 |
| 11. | 10 Commandments Exodus 20 | 24. James 1:5–6 |
| 12. | Romans 8:37–39 | 25. Isaiah 12:2 |
| 13. | 1 Corinthians 13:4–7 | 26. 1 John 3:23 |

| Level Three | | | |
|---|---|---|---|
| 1. | John 3:16-17 | 14. | Ephesians 4:29–30 |
| 2. | Matthew 28:19-20 | 15. | James 1:26–27 |
| 3. | Philippians 4:8 | 16. | John 15:5–8 |
| 4. | Leviticus 18:4–5 | 17. | Corinthians 9:26–27 |
| 5. | Mark 13:32–33 | 18. | John 10:8–11 |
| 6. | Romans 12:14–16 | 19. | Romans 10:9–13 |
| 7. | Galatians 6:14–15 | 20. | 1 Peter 1:13–16 |
| 8. | John 13:34–35 | 21. | Colossians 3:12–14 |
| 9. | Philippians 1:20–21 | 22. | Proverbs 31:8–9 |
| 10. | Isaiah 45:22–24 | 23. | Matthew 16:24–26 |
| 11. | 1 John 4:11–12 | 24. | Ephesians 2:8–10 |
| 12. | Deuteronomy 5:32–33 | 25. | Psalms 96:9–10 |
| 13. | Leviticus 23:3 | 26. | Romans 12:9–13 |

The Absolute Basics of Christianity is a Bible study workbook designed for believers at all stages of spiritual growth and maturity. These lessons can be used in small groups or as a self-study for those who desire to learn more about their faith and take a fresh look at the basics of the Christian faith. Each week's lessons center around one basic theme of the Christian faith. The weekly topics for volume one include, Assurance of Salvation, Baptism, Church, Discipleship, Evangelism, Forgiveness, Gifts, Heaven and Hell, I Am, Joy, Kingdom, Love, and Money. The topics in volume two are, New Life, Obedience, Prayer, Quiet Time, Revelation, Spirit, Trinity, Unity, Victory, Worthy Walk, 10 Commandments, Yield, and Zelotes. Each topic is further broken down into four individual lessons that are jam-packed with Scripture references. This will challenge readers to explore God's Word with their own Bibles. The Absolute Basics of Christianity's twenty-six week study is Biblically centered Theologically enlightening Spiritually engaging. By the end of this study, students will have memorized passages of Scripture and learned Bible study techniques, along with self-discipline. They will also know how to share their faith and be able to explain what they believe to others. Furthermore, through the process of looking up Scripture in their own Bibles, students who are unfamiliar with the Bible will learn to navigate their way through God's Word. Thousands have used The Absolute Basics of Christianity to gain confidence, knowledge, and the ability to explain their faith to those who have yet to believe. All believers who desire to grow and mature in their faith should consider completing the lessons in The Absolute Basics of Christianity at some point in their Christian walk.

*This workbook can be purchased at*
**www.pastorpete.org** *or* **www.amazon.com.**

Made in the USA
Charleston, SC
14 February 2015